Understanding Core French Grammar

Andrew Betts

Lancing College, England

Vernon Series in Language and Linguistics

www.vernonpress.com

In the Americas:
Vernon Press
1000 N West Street,
Suite 1200, Wilmington,
Delaware 19801
United States

In the rest of the world:
Vernon Press
C/Sancti Espiritu 17,
Malaga, 29006
Spain

Vernon Series in Language and Linguistics

Library of Congress Control Number: 2016947126

ISBN: 978-1-62273-069-8

Product and company names mentioned in this work are the trademarks of their respective owners. While every care has been taken in preparing this work, neither the authors nor Vernon Art and Science Inc. may be held responsible for any loss or damage caused or alleged to be caused directly or indirectly by the information contained in it.

Table of Contents

Acknowledgements

This book has evolved from teaching notes made over the last 25 years and I am grateful to the many pupils at Lancing College whom I have taught and who have enabled me to develop this work. I would like to thank Dan Brooks and Henry Smethurst in particular who have taken the trouble to read through much of this material. Equally I would like to thank my colleagues Laura Fryer and Sylvain Baudet for their comments and encouragement. I would like to thank Hannah for extreme proof-reading, suggestions to improve style as well as content and for being my sternest critic! Professor Jacques Durand deserves a special mention for encouraging me to acknowledge that language exists primarily as a spoken medium in the real world. Finally my thanks are due to the late Brian Day who inspired me to learn French many years ago at Sutton Valence School.

All errors and omissions are, of course, my responsibility.

For EB and JHRB with thanks and love

AJB

Lancing

May 2016

Introduction

The purpose of this book is to explain how the core systems of French grammar work and to try to make mastering the language easier for the English-speaking learner. It deals with verbs and verb constructions, pronouns and their use, adjectives, adverbs and articles and concludes with a section on the primacy of the spoken language.

The idea is to give as few lists as possible except where really necessary, as with the irregular present tenses for example, and these lists are given in appendices at the back of the book. Instead the main part of the book focuses on explaining the systems which need to be tackled in order to understand and master the language.

Chapter 1 covers the tenses of French and tries to simplify the problem of mastering and learning the detail. Chapter 2 considers and explains verb processes and constructions. Chapter 3 concerns the system of French pronouns. There is a discussion of subjects and objects in general and then we look at the whole range of pronouns and their behaviour in French and how to use them, giving extensive worked examples. Chapter 4 looks at issues surrounding adjectives, adverbs and articles. For each of Chapters 1 to 4, there are exercises corresponding to each topic covered at the end of the book

Chapter 5 is different in nature, drawing the learner's attention to the reality of language, which is primarily a spoken medium. It points out that the system and detail given so far describes a formal, official version of the language. Considering just the three areas of negation, questions and passives it highlights the fact that the world of real spoken French can differ greatly from the standard given in the rest of the book. There are of course very many other ways in which the real world differs from the text book.

It should be noted here that this book is not intended for the complete beginner. Although I do treat some very basic issues as well as more complicated ones, a knowledge of fundamental grammatical processes and principles is assumed.

Tense Formation

1.0 Tenses – Summary

This section is a summary of the basic tenses of French which are considered in more detail in sections 2-8 in this chapter.

1.1 Simple (One-Word) Tenses:

<u>Present</u>   **Regular:**   *-er*   *-ir*   *-re*

e	*ons*	*is*	*issons*	*s*	*ons*
es	*ez*	*is*	*issez*	*s*	*ez*
e	*ent*	*it*	*issent*	*-*	*ent*

Irregular: There is a list of the 48 most common irregular present tense verbs in appendix 1. Learn them – this is the hardest thing you will have to do.

<u>Imperfect</u>   **Regular:**   If you learn all the irregular present tenses, all verbs except *être* are regular in the imperfect because they all form their stem by removing the *ons* from the *nous* form of the present tense and adding the imperfect endings which are:

ais	*ions*
ais	*iez*
ait	*aient*

Irregular:	The stem for the only irregular imperfect verb *être* is:
	ét-

Future **Regular:** The stem for the future tense for *–er* and *–ir* verbs is the infinitive itself. The stem for *–re* verbs is the infinitive without the final *–e*.

Irregular: There are about 20 common irregular stems. You just have to learn them. The list is in Chapter 1 section 4.0. For both regular and irregular verbs you just have to add the following endings:

ai	*ons*
as	*ez*
a	*ont*

Conditional **Regular:** Add the imperfect endings to the future stem.

Because you will have learned the irregular future stems and the imperfect endings, there are no irregular conditionals.

1.2 Compound (Two-Word) Tenses:

<u>Perfect or Passé Composé</u>

There are three things which you need to know in order to get this right:

i)   Past participle (see Chapter 1 section 5.0 and appendix 2)
ii) Which auxiliary – *avoir/être*? (see Chapter 1 section 5.0)
iii) Agreement Rules (see Chapter 1 section 6.0)

Regular:

Past Participle for *-er* verbs → *é*

Past Participle for *-ir* verbs → *i*

Past Participle for *-re* verbs → *u*

Irregular:

There are about 48 common irregular past participles which you just have to learn. The list is in appendix 2.

Once you have mastered this, you have also done almost everything you need to do in order to master three more tenses – pluperfect, future perfect and conditional perfect. You just need to change the tense of the auxiliary (aux).

Perfect	*J'ai* (present aux) *fini*	*I have finished*
Pluperfect	*J'avais* (imperfect aux) *fini*	*I had finished*
Future Perfect	*J'aurai* (future aux) *fini*	*I will have finished*
Conditional Perfect	*J'aurais* (conditional aux) *fini*	*I would have finished*

Simply by changing the tense of the auxiliary, you get the rest of these tenses for free. You use the same past participles and the same agreement rules apply. See Chapter 1 section 7.0 for a further discussion of these extra tenses.

2.0 Present Tense

2.1 Regular Verbs

The present tense is the most complicated of the tenses in that there are three different sets of endings for the three different sorts of regular verbs, the *–er, -ir* and *-re* verbs.

The endings are:

Present:	**Regular**	*-er*		*-ir*		*-re*	
		e	*ons*	*is*	*issons*	*s*	*ons*
		es	*ez*	*is*	*issez*	*s*	*ez*
		e	*ent*	*it*	*issent*	*-*	*ent*

To form the tense just remove the *–er, -ir* or *–re* from the end of the infinitive and add the above endings in the appropriate person and number. Here are some examples for the regular verbs *jouer, finir* and *vendre*:

You (singular) play/are playing	*Tu joues*
We finish/are finishing	*Nous finissons*
They sell/are selling	*Ils/elles vendent*

If you learn the endings then formation of the present tense regulars is pretty straightforward apart from a few stem spelling changes in the *–er* verbs for the *je, tu, il/elle/on* and *ils/elles* forms only:

i)   Verbs ending in *-eler* and *–eter* double the consonant, eg *j'appelle* but *nous appelons*;

ii)   In some verbs such as *acheter* the stem *e* becomes *è*, eg *il achète* but *vous achetez*;

iii)   The *é* in *espérer* changes to *è*, eg *tu espères* but *nous espérons*;

iv)   *–ger* verbs such as *manger* retain the *e* after the *g* in the *nous* form, eg *nous mangeons*;

v)   In *-cer* verbs such as *commencer* the *c* becomes *ç* in the *nous* form, eg *nous commençons*.

All of these changes simply reflect changes in pronunciation. With the verbs which double the consonant or change accent, the spelling change is needed because the stem vowel is the final pronounced syllable in the *je, tu, il/elle/on* and *ils/elles* forms and cannot be the weak *e* or the bright *é* sound. In the *nous* and *vous* forms the stem vowel is followed by a pronounced syllable *-ons* or *-ez* allowing the stem vowel to be pronounced in the same way as in the infinitive, leaving the stem vowel either weak as in *appeler* or able to be pronounced with the brighter sound of the acute accent as in *espérer*.

In the *-ger* and *-cer* verbs, the spelling change happens in order to 'soften' the *g* and *c* respectively. Without this they would be pronounced with their hard equivalents as in *grand* or *couteau*. In all of the other forms of the *-cer* verbs there is already an *e* after the *c* to soften the consonant.

2.2 Irregular verbs

Irregular verbs just have to be learned. There is a list of the 48 most common of them in appendix 1. Pick them off one by one. Learning the present tense makes the imperfect tense very easy! See Chapter 1 section 3.0.

2.3 Difficulties with the Present Tense

English has two forms of each tense, the simple and the continuous, and French only has one. So *I swim* and *I am swimming* are both translated by *je nage* and there just is no equivalent of the continuous in French in the present tense or in fact in any tense.

Equally in both Questions and Negation in English the support verb *do* is used and again, this just does not happen in French where the usual tense of the verb is used. So *I do not swim* becomes *je ne nage pas* (See Chapter 2 section 4.0) and *do you swim?* is *nages-tu?* or *est-ce que tu nages?* (see Chapter 2 section 3.0).

Also, sometimes in English we use the verb *do* for emphasis for example in *I **do** understand*. This just does not happen in French where some other phrase such as *en effet* might be used as in *en effet, je comprends*.

I have not included a separate regular present tense section of sentences for translation into French. However, there are some examples in the Tense Chart sentences.

3.0 Imperfect Tense

As mentioned in Chapter 1 section 1.0 in the tense summary, the imperfect tense is very easy to form **if** you know the present tense of a verb. This is a very good reason why you should learn all of the irregular present tense verbs that you can.

What is needed to form the imperfect tense is a stem and a set of endings. These details are given in Chapter 1 section 1.1 but are repeated here for convenience. The stem is found by going to the *nous* form of the present tense and removing the *-ons* ending. For example:

Nous allons	→	*all-*
Nous prenons	→	*pren-*
Nous buvons	→	*buv-*
Nous finissons	→	*finiss-*
Nous vendons	→	*vend-*
Nous jouons	→	*jou-*

The only exception to this is *être* because there is no *–ons* on the *nous* form of this verb because it is *nous sommes*! The only irregular stem for the imperfect then is *ét-* for *être*.

The endings for the imperfect are:

ais	*ions*
ais	*iez*
ait	*aient*

and these have to be added to the appropriate stem.

The imperfect is used to talk about habits and states in the past in French and there is a discussion of how to use it compared to the use of the perfect tense, which is used to talk about single events or acts in the past, in Chapter 1 section 8.0.

The imperfect in French will always be used to translate the continuous version of the English imperfect as well as the construction involving *used to*:

> *We were going to the beach* *Nous allions à la plage*
> *We used to play tennis* *Nous jouions au tennis*

I have not included a separate section of exercises on the imperfect but you can look at the Tense Chart sentences where there are one or two sentences which test this issue.

4.0 Future Tense and Conditional Tense

Future Tense

For the future tense you just need a set of endings, which are the same for all verbs, and a stem. The endings are:

> -ai   -ons
>
> -as   -ez
>
> -a   -ont

The stem for the **regular verbs** is found by going to the last 'r' on the infinitive; for -er and -ir verbs it is the infinitive itself and for -re verbs you just need to remove the final -e. For example:

> *jouer*   *je jouerai*   *I will play*
>
> *finir*   *elle finira*   *she will finish*
>
> *vendre*   *nous vendrons*   *we will sell*

Learn the following **<u>irregular</u>** future stems, then you can form almost all common future tenses:

aller	*to go*	*ir-*
s'asseoir	*to sit down*	*s'assiér-*
avoir	*to have*	*aur-*
courir	*to run*	*courr-*
devoir	*must/to have to*	*devr-*
envoyer	*to send*	*enverr-*
être	*to be*	*ser-*
faire	*to do*	*fer-*
falloir	*to be necessary*	*faudr-*
mourir	*to die*	*mourr-*
pleuvoir	*to rain*	*pleuvr- (il form only)*
pouvoir	*can/to be able*	*pourr-*
recevoir	*to receive*	*recevr*
savoir	*to know*	*saur-*
tenir	*to hold*	*tiendr-*
valoir	*to be worth*	*vaudr-*
venir	*to come*	*viendr-*
voir	*to see*	*verr-*
vouloir	*to want*	*voudr*

Conditional Tense:

The conditional tense is formed by using the future stem and adding the imperfect tense endings to it instead of the future tense endings. The imperfect tense endings are:

-ais	*-ions*
-ais	*-iez*
-ait	*-aient*

So:

jouer	*je jouer**ais***	*I would play*
finir	*elle finir**ait***	*she would finish*
vendre	*nous vendr**ions***	*we would sell*

5.0 Perfect Tense

The perfect tense in French, which is also known as the *passé composé*, is a past tense. It is the tense you use whenever you want to say something like:

> We **have read** the book   *Nous **avons lu** le livre*
>
> They **have been reading**   *Ils **ont lu***

It is also used sometimes to translate the single word English past tense verbs like:

> She **wrote** *a letter*   *Elle **a écrit** une lettre*
>
> I **ate** *the toast*   *J'**ai mangé** le pain grillé*

It is only used to translate this sort of <u>single word</u> past tense when what happened was an <u>event</u> or a <u>single act</u>. Otherwise you use the imperfect tense (see the Tense Chart in Chapter 1 section 8.0 for fuller details).

Formation Basics

You always need two parts to form this tense. You have to use the <u>present tense of</u> <u>*avoir* (to have)</u> or <u>*être* (to be)</u>, along with the <u>past participle</u> of the main verb.

> *Elle a fini*   *She finished / she has finished*
>
> *Il est venu*   *He came / he has come*

For regular verbs, you get the past participle by removing the *–er, -ir* or *-re* from the infinitive and adding *-é, -i* or *-u* respectively:

> *Jouer - to play*   →   *jou**é***
>
> *Finir - to finish*   →   *fin**i***
>
> *Vendre - to sell*   →   *vend**u***

There are some irregular past participles and you just have to learn them. There is a list of them in appendix 2.

Avoir Verbs:

Most verbs use the present tense of *avoir* which is just like what happens in the English perfect:

J'ai	*Nous avons*
Tu as	*Vous avez*
Il/elle a	*Ils/elles ont*

Être Verbs:

Some verbs use the present tense of *être* and this looks a little bit odd but you just have to learn them and think when using them:

Je suis	*Nous sommes*
Tu es	*Vous êtes*
Il/elle est	*Ils/elles sont*

The verbs which need *être* are often called the **DRAPERS VAN MMT 13** to help you remember them. They are:

Infinitive	Meaning	Past Participle
Descendre	*to go down*	*descendu*
Rester	*to stay*	*resté*
Aller	*to go*	*allé*
Partir	*to leave*	*parti*
Entrer	*to enter*	*entré*
Retourner	*to return*	*retourné*
Sortir	*to go out*	*sorti*
Venir	*to come*	*venu*
Arriver	*to arrive*	*arrivé*
Naître	*to be born*	*né*
Mourir	*to die*	*mort*
Monter	*to climb*	*monté*
Tomber	*to fall*	*tombé*

There are 13 of them. There are some agreement rules which need to be explained in order to complete the picture and these are given in Chapter 1 section 6.0 immediately below. Compounds of these verbs such as *repartir, parvenir, redescendre* etc also take *être*.

Reflexive Verbs

In the perfect tense and in the other compound tenses, all reflexive verbs take *être*:

*Je **me** suis lavé*   *Nous **nous** sommes lavés*

*Tu **t'**es lavé*   *Vous **vous** êtes lavés*

*Il **s'**est lavé*   *Ils **se** sont lavés*

*Elle **s'**est lavée*   *Elles **se** sont lavées*

Any *avoir* verb which can have an object can also be reflexive and will then take *être*:

*Il **a** vu la fille*   *He saw the girl*

but

*Il **s'est** vu dans le mirroir*   *He saw himself in the mirror*

and here the verb *voir* which takes *avoir* in the perfect takes *être* as soon as it is used reflexively.

6.0 Compound Tense Past Participle Agreement

In this section we look at agreement of the past participle with either the subject with *être* verbs or with the **p**receding **d**irect **o**bject (**PDO**) with *avoir* and reflexive verbs.

6.1 *Être* Verbs

With the verbs which take *être*, there is agreement of the past participle with the subject: add nothing for masculine singular, *e* for feminine singular, *s* for masculine or mixed plural and *es* for feminine plural:

> *Elle* (feminine singular) *est arrivée*
>
> *Il* (masculine singular) *est monté*
>
> *Elles* (feminine plural) *sont allées*
>
> *Nous* (masculine or mixed plural) *sommes partis*

6.2 *Avoir* Verbs

With the verbs which take *avoir* there is agreement with the preceding direct object if there is one. This means that the object must come **before** the verb and it must be a **direct** object. Consider *J'ai vu les filles.* Here, the direct object *les filles* is after the verb and so there is no agreement. If you turn the direct object into a pronoun *les,* (see Chapter 3 section 2.2) which still refers to the girls and so still is feminine, we then have a PDO and so there is feminine agreement shown by adding *es*: *Je les ai vues.*

If the preceding object is indirect there is no agreement, eg *Je leur ai donné le livre.* Here *leur* is a preceding object and although it is plural, there is no agreement because it is an indirect object, the **goal** in the transaction of **giving**.

There are three main sorts of constructions where there might be a PDO:

i)   where there is a pronoun object of a verb as in the example given *Je les ai vues*;

ii)   Where there is a relative clause introduced by the object relative pronoun *que,* eg *La femme que j'ai vue – the woman that I saw*. In this clause, we are talking about **a woman whom I have seen**. I did the seeing and **the woman** is the thing that **I saw** and although it is not in the usual object place, after the verb for a full noun in French, it still is the direct object and it comes in front of the verb and so is a PDO. So these *que* object relative clauses are another context where PDO agreement is almost certain to happen when the verb is in a compound tense (perfect, pluperfect, etc). See Chapter 3 section 3.1 for details on relative pronouns;

iii)   where there is a 'wh-' question which asks for information about a specific noun and it is the object of the verb, eg *Quelle table as-tu achetée?* (see section on Question formation in Chapter 2 section 3.0). Here we are asking **Which table did you buy/have you bought? You** did the buying and **the table** is the thing that you bought. So again the direct object is not in the usual place for a full noun object and comes in front of the verb, making this another context in which PDO agreement must happen.

6.3 Agreement in Reflexive Verbs

This is an odd one because reflexive verbs in French take *être* as their auxiliary and you would think that they should agree with their subject as with the ordinary *être* verbs as in 6.1 above. In fact in 90% of cases it looks just as if this is happening.

However, reflexive verbs in compound tenses take *être* but their past participles agree with the preceding direct object if there is one. In *les filles se sont levées* the reflexive pronoun *se* is the direct object of the verb *lever*. The girls 'raised' themselves. In the same way *la main* is direct object when *lever* is used with a full noun object, as in *il a levé la main – he raised his hand*.

However in *elle s'est donné un cadeau* where *cadeau - present* is the direct object of the verb *donner – to give*, the *s'* is the indirect object of the verb *donner* and the sentence means *she gave herself a present*. In this sentence there is no agreement on the past participle because the *s'* which does indeed precede the verb is in fact an **indirect** object meaning *to herself*. These indirect object reflexive pronouns are actually quite rare.

When this sort of agreement does happen it is really just the same sort of agreement as ordinary PDO agreement with *avoir* verbs. There is one sentence in the exercises on compound tense agreement which tests you on this.

7.0 The Further Compound Tenses

As mentioned earlier, once you have mastered the perfect tense, three other tenses are immediately available to you. The pluperfect, future perfect and the conditional perfect are made in exactly the same way as the perfect tense except that the tense of the auxiliary verb (the bit of *avoir/être*) changes. Here they are along with the perfect:

Perfect	*J'ai* (present aux) *fini*	*I have finished*
Pluperfect	*J'avais* (imperfect aux) *fini*	*I had finished*
Future Perfect	*J'aurai* (future aux) *fini*	*I will have finished*
Conditional Perfect	*J'aurais* (conditional aux) *fini*	*I would have finished*

The same verbs use *être*, the irregular past participles are the same and the agreement rules for the past participle are the same.

The **pluperfect** is formed using the imperfect of *avoir/être* with the past participle and corresponds to **had** *done/swum/written/gone* in English. For example:

She had eaten	→	*Elle avait mangé*
We had finished	→	*Nous avions fini*
They had arrived	→	*Ils étaient arrivés*

The **future perfect** using the future of *avoir/être* with the past participle and corresponds to ***will have*** *done/swum/written/gone* in English. For example:

She will have eaten	→	*Elle aura mangé*
We will have finished	→	*Nous aurons fini*
They will have arrived	→	*Ils seront arrivés*

The **conditional perfect** using the conditional of *avoir/être* with the past participle and corresponds to ***would have*** *done/swam/written/gone* in English. For example:

She would have eaten	→	*Elle aurait mangé*
We would have finished	→	*Nous aurions fini*
They would have arrived	→	*Ils seraient arrivés*

If you can recognise and identify these tenses in English, then putting them into French should be easy because they are in fact formed in exactly the same way. The only slight problem is remembering to use *être* with the **DRAPERS VAN MMT 13** verbs because you might feel that it sounds odd, but *elle **serait** partie* does mean *she would have left* for example. Also you have to follow the same agreement rules as for the perfect tense.

8.0 Tense Chart

Present:

I play

I am playing — *Je joue* — **Présent**

Perfect:

I have played

I have been playing — *J'ai joué* — **Passé composé**

Once/event

Imperfect:

I played

State/Habit

I was playing — *Je jouais* — **Imparfait**
(I used to play)

Pluperfect:

I had played

I had been playing — *J'avais joué* — **Plus que parfait**

Future:

I will play

I will be playing — *Je jouerai* — **Futur**

Conditional:

I would play

I would be playing — *Je jouerais* — **Conditionel**

N.B There are two versions of each English Tense but only one French version.

As you can see from the chart, going from English to French we go to a system which has half the number of forms. On the English side, there are two forms for each tense. The first of each pair is called the SIMPLE and the second is called the CONTINUOUS and is made up of the verb *to be* in the same tense as the simple version along with the main verb + *ing*, for example:

> *I sing*
>
> *I am singing*

There are no continuous forms in French.

The only complicated spot is when you have a past tense which is a single word in English - the imperfect tense. Here you have to use your brain and decide if the action was **Once or an Event**, or whether it was **a State or Habit**. You can use this chart to decide how to get the right tense of any verb, apart from the exceptions discussed below. So always keep it with you when you are writing.

There are a couple of exceptions to the chart.

Time expressions in the perfect or pluperfect in English with *for*: English uses the perfect or pluperfect tense with these expressions where French uses present or imperfect. For example, *I have lived here for 4 years*. Here French uses the present tense plus *depuis*, eg *j'habite ici depuis 4 ans*. The same sort of thing goes on with pluperfect expressions with *for*, for example, *I had lived there for 4 years* where in French they use the imperfect with *depuis* eg *j'habitais là depuis 4 ans*.

Which tense to use after *when/quand*: in English after *when*, most frequently we use present tense and perfect tense, eg *I will do that when **I am** ready* or *I will do that when **I have finished**.* However, the tense in French after *when* is different. The English present tense becomes French future tense and the English perfect becomes French future perfect (meaning *will have finished*). So these will be: *je ferai ça quand je serai prêt* and *je ferai ça quand j'aurai fini*.

The reason for this is that the French follows the time of the tense more precisely. In the first one, where English uses the present tense, the fact is that the person is not ready and so it seems odd in French to use the present tense which is used for comment on present time where in fact we are talking about a future state of readiness.

It is the same sort of thing in the second example where English uses the perfect tense. French uses the perfect tense for completed actions in the past and this action is clearly not finished but will be at some time and it is not in the past so they use the future perfect.

9.0 Past Historic

The past historic (PH) is a purely literary tense and as such you do not need to know how to use it unless you intend to write novels in French. Nonetheless it is important to be able to recognise it when reading French novels and stories. So here are the basics of its formation.

For *–er* verbs take the *nous* form of the present tense and remove the *–ons,* then add:

ai	*âmes*
as	*âtes*
a	*èrent*

For verbs whose past participle ends in *–i, –is,* or *–it,* use the following endings based on the stem of the past participle:

is	*îmes*
is	*îtes*
it	*irent*

These endings are also used for the past historic of *faire – je fis, tu fis,* etc.

For some verbs whose past participle ends in *–u,* use the following endings:

us	*ûmes*
us	*ûtes*
ut	*urent*

However, there are several verbs which have *–u* past participles (PP) which do not follow this pattern and amongst them are the following:

i)   verbs whose infinitives end in *–andre, -ondre, -endre* and *–rdre*

répandre	*to spread*	*PP répandu*	*PH je répandis – I spread*
répondre	*to reply*	*PP répondu*	*PH je répondis – I replied*
entendre	*to hear*	*PP entendu*	*PH j'entendis – I heard*
perdre	*to lose*	*PP perdu*	*PH je perdis – I lost*

ii)   the following, which either follow the *–is* pattern or are just irregular and have to be learned:

battre	*battis*
vaincre	*vanquis*
coudre	*cousis*
tenir	*tins*
venir	*vins*
vêtir	*vêtis*
voir	*vis*

There are of course others such as *être* and *avoir* which go: *fus, fus, fut, fûmes, fûtes, furent* and *eus, eus, eut, eûmes, eûtes, eurent* respectively.

When translating into English they just translate to the simple past tense, so:

il fut	*he was*
ils allèrent	*they went*
etc	

10.0 Past Anterior

Like the past historic the past anterior is a purely literary tense and again as such you do not need to know how to use it unless you intend to write novels in French. Nonetheless it is important to be able to recognise it when reading French novels and stories. So here are the basics of its formation and use.

It is the literary equivalent of the pluperfect and is only used in very specific contexts. Firstly its English equivalent is a pluperfect. Secondly, it is introduced by one of the following conjunctions:

après que	*after*
aussitôt que	*as soon as*
dès que	*as soon as*
lorsque	*when*
quand	*when*

Thirdly, the verb following it has to express an action or event and so will be in the past historic.

It is formed very simply by using the past historic of the auxiliary verb *avoir* or *être*, according to the usual rules for the choice of auxiliary, along with the past participle, exactly in the same way as when forming any compound tense. Also the same agreement rules apply (see Chapter 1 section 6.0 on compound tense agreement).

Here are some examples with the necessary conditions highlighted:

> **Après qu'elle fut arrivée** *à la gare elle* **prit** *le train de dix heures*
> *After she had arrived at the station she took the 10 o'clock train*

> **Quand** *mon frère* **eut fini** *d'écrire la lettre il* **alla** *à la poste*
> *When my brother had finished writing the letter he went to the post office*

As said, you do not need to be able to produce this tense. It is just useful to be able to recognise it when reading novels.

Chapter 2

Verb Constructions

1.0 Passives

People get in a twist about passives in French when they do not need to at all. You just have to understand what is going on in your own language first and then (almost) completely replicate the process in French.

Passives in English

The following is an Active/Passive pair and we will base what we do on this:

Active: *Fred ate the chicken*
Passive: *The chicken was eaten (by Fred)*

These two sentences are linked by an entirely regular process which will turn any active sentence into a passive one.

```
        4    3    1
Active:  Fred ate  the chicken
Passive: The chicken was eaten (by Fred)
          1      2    3      4
```

Step 1:   Original active object becomes passive subject
Step 2:   Insert the verb *to be* in the same tense as the active main verb
Step 3:   Convert the original main verb into its past participle
Step 4:   Move the original active subject into an optional 'by-phrase'

Using this formula for English, you can create a passive sentence from any sentence in which the verb has an object.

Passives in French

The following is the same Active/Passive pair in French:

Active: *Fred a mangé le poulet*
Passive: *Le poulet a été mangé (par Fred)*

These two sentences are linked by almost entirely the same process as in English:

```
             4       3       1
```
Active: *Fred a mangé le poulet*
Passive: *Le poulet a été mangé (par Fred)*
```
             1       2       3       4
```

Step 1:   Original active **direct** object becomes passive subject
Step 2:   Insert the verb *être* in the same tense as the active main verb
Step 3:   Convert the original main verb into its past participle
Step 4:   Move the original active subject into an optional *'par*-phrase'

There are some differences between the English and French passive process of course.

Firstly, in step 1 in French I have stipulated that passives have to be made from 'original active **direct** object'. This of course means that active **indirect** objects, in other words 'à-phrases', cannot become passive subjects. So where in English we can have both a) *a letter was sent to us (by X)* and b) *we were sent a letter (by X)* from *X sent us a letter*, from the equivalent French active *X nous a envoyé une lettre*, we can only get *une lettre nous a été envoyée*, the equivalent of the English a), and there is no passive equivalent of the English passive b). This is the trickiest thing to get to grips with in French passives. The way they express some equivalent to b) is to keep it active and use the impersonal pronoun *on*: *on nous a envoyé une lettre*.

Secondly, and this is easy, you must agree the passive past participle with the passive subject as in the example above: *une lettre nous a été envoyée*. Apart from this you just need to get the tenses right.

Actually, French uses passives far less often that English does, very frequently using the *on* plus active option instead or sometimes using reflexive constructions. See Chapter 2 section 6.0 on reflexives for more detail and Chapter 5 section 3 for a discussion of real language use.

2.0 Imperatives

Imperatives are commands such as *Open the door, Sit down* or *Let's go!* In French they are easy to form.

There are three different main sorts of imperative in French; second person singular or the *tu* form of the verb, second person plural or the *vous* form of the verb, and first person plural or *nous* form of the verb. English does not make a difference between singular and plural *you* forms but we do have the first person plural imperative as in *Let's go!* above.

To form the imperative, simply take the *tu, vous* or *nous* form of the verb. For example:

Take the book	*Prends le livre*
Eat your salad	*Mangez votre salade*
Let's go home	*Rentrons à la maison*

There is just one irregularity which is that *–er* verb second person singular or *tu* imperatives remove the *–s* at the end. In fact all verbs which end in *–es* or *–as* remove the *–s*. For example:

Play well!	*Joue bien!*
Go to the end	*Va à la fin*

A slightly irritating twist to this is that when they are followed by *y* or *en*, the *–s* returns, for example:

Go on/there	*Vas-y*
Eat some	*Manges-en*

We need to say a few words about imperatives and pronouns (see Chapter 3 section 2.3.2 also). Normally, when not using an imperative, object pronouns such as *le, la* and *les* have to go in front of the verb as in *Je la vois – I see her.* However, positive commands are the exception and the object pronouns come after the verb, for example:

Eat it!	*Mange-le!*
Catch her!	*Attrape-la!*

Also in these positive commands, the non-stressable object pronouns *me* and *te* are replaced by their stressable equivalents *moi* and *toi*. For example:

> *Give me the book*   *Donnez-moi le livre*

As you can see too, all of these pronouns which come after the verb in positive commands are linked to the verb by a hyphen.

In negative commands the pronouns go in their usual position in front of the verb, and we use the usual non-stressable versions, for example:

> *Don't give me the book*   *Ne me donnez pas le livre*
> *Don't eat it*   *Ne le mange pas*
> *Don't catch her*   *Ne l'attrape pas*

Imperatives of reflexive verbs follow the same rules. For example:

> *Wash yourself*   *Lavez-vous*
> *Don't wash yourself*   *Ne vous lavez pas*
> *Get up*   *Lève-toi*
> *Don't get up*   *Ne te lève pas*

Occasionally plain infinitives can be used as imperatives but this is only in formulaic, written instructions.

3.0 Questions

We should talk a little here about questions in English first.

There are two basic sorts of question:

i)   **Yes/No** questions to which the answer *yes* or *no* is appropriate, for example *Do you play the piano?*

ii)   **Wh-** questions which expect an answer with rather more information in them such as place, time, reason etc, for example *Why do you play the piano?* They can be called **Wh-** questions because they are usually introduced by words such as *Where, When* or *Why*.

In French quite naturally there are the same two types of questions, with the equivalent of most **Wh-** words beginning in *Qu-* and so we could call them **Qu-** questions. We will come back to these later.

Likewise, there are two different ways of **making** questions in English:

i)   Sometimes we use the auxiliary verb *do* in different tenses with the main verb to make these. For example *Do you like chicken?* is created from the statement *You like chicken* by introducing the verb *do* in the appropriate tense and agreeing with the subject.

ii)   The other way does not use *do* because there is already a modal or other auxiliary verb such as *may, can, will, would* etc. For example *May I go now?* or *Would you like a cup of tea?* The verb *to be* does not use *do* although the verb *to have* does sometimes.

You will be very pleased to hear that although there are also two ways of building questions in French the situation is much simpler.

i)   Firstly, if the subject is a pronoun simply invert the subject and verb. So, *Tu aimes le poulet* becomes *Aimes-tu le poulet?* where there is a hyphen between the subject and the verb. If the subject is a full noun or noun phrase such as *the president* you cannot use this method. If the subject is the pronoun *il* or *elle*, we need to insert *-t-* between the inverted verb and the subject to make it pronounceable, eg *Aime-t-il le poulet?*

ii)   Secondly, the other option which can be used regardless of what the subject is, pronoun or full noun, is to put *Est-ce que* in front of the statement. So, using this method, *Tu aimes le poulet* becomes *Est-ce que tu aimes le poulet?* By the way, *Est-ce que?* just means quite literally *Is it that?*

Some of the **Qu-** words in French are the following (although you can see that not all begin in *Qu)*:

qui	*who*
comment	*how/what (like what in comment t'appelles-tu?)*
quand	*when*
pourquoi	*why*
où	*where*
quel*	*which*
d'où	*from where*
combien	*how much/how many*

  * *Quel* has four different forms for masculine/feminine, singular/plural:

	Masc	Fem
Singular	*Quel*	*Quelle*
Plural	*Quels*	*Quelles*

Eg   *Quelle chemise as-tu achetée?*   *Which shirt did you buy ?*
       Quels matchs as-tu regardés?   *Which matches did you watch ?*

So, to make the **Yes/No** questions in French just use one of the two strategies above. To make the **Qu-** questions simply put the **Qu-** word in front of the questions; for example, as we have seen, *Tu aimes le poulet* can become *Aimes-tu le poulet?* or *Est-ce que tu aimes le poulet?* To ask **why** someone likes chicken, simply bolt *pourquoi* onto the front of these **Yes/No** questions, giving *Pourquoi aimes-tu le poulet?* or *Pourquoi est-ce que tu aimes le poulet?*

Questions with prepositions

In English we can have prepositions left dangling at the end of sentences, although not all speakers of English think that this is acceptable. So for example we can say *Who did you go to the party with?* This seems pretty normal even though some (old-fashioned) speakers would prefer *With who(m) did you go to the party?* This latter option, however, is what we have to do in French. You just cannot leave prepositions dangling in French and so this question will have to be *Avec qui es-tu allé à la boum?* and so on. So *Who did you buy that for?* would be *Pour qui as-tu acheté ça?* See Chapter 5 section 2 for a look at question formation in spoken French.

See Chapter 3 section 4.0 for more on interrogative pronouns.

4.0 Negation

We should begin by talking about negation in English first.

Just as with questions, there are two different ways of negating a sentence in English:

i)   In the first method, used with the majority of verbs, again we use the auxiliary verb *do*. This is introduced in the appropriate tense and the word *not* is placed after it and followed by the main verb in its infinitive form without the *to*. So the affirmative *I know* becomes *I do not know*.

ii)   As with question formation, the second method involves the auxiliary verb or modal such as *may, can, will, would* etc. Again this includes *to be* but not always the verb *to have* and again the verb *do* is not used. Instead the negative particle *not* is placed directly after the auxiliary verb. So the affirmative *I will buy a car* becomes *I will not buy a car*, and so on.

In French, there is only one method of forming negatives regardless of the verb type. Quite simply, the negative particle *ne* is placed in front of the tensed verb and the 'negative completer', for which there are several possibilities, is placed after the tensed verb. So for example *J'aime le poulet* becomes *Je n'aime **pas** le poulet*. Here the negative completer is the most common, *pas*, which just has the force of *not* in English.

It is important to underline that the negative elements go around the tensed verb and not any past participle or dependent infinitives, so for example *J'ai vu mes amis* becomes *Je **n'ai pas** vu mes amis* where the past participle *vu* is outside the 'negative envelope'. Similarly, with modal verbs (see Chapter 2 section 8.0 for a further discussion of Modal verbs) such as *pouvoir*, the dependent infinitive is outside the negative envelope. So *Il peut finir le repas* becomes *Il **ne** peut **pas** finir le repas*.

It is worth noting at this point that if there are any pronoun objects in front of the verb then they too are included inside the negative envelope. Thus *Je les ai vus* becomes *Je **ne** les ai **pas** vus*.

Another point is that you will almost never have *un/une* after *pas* or any other negative completer. See Chapter 4 section 3.2.2 for the exception. Instead you will use *de*. So *J'ai un frère* will become *Je n'ai pas **de** frère*.

The only time where the *ne* and *pas* appear next to each other is when an infinitive is being negated. So *Il est important de fumer* becomes *il est important de **ne pas** fumer*. This also happens where there is a pronoun object and so *il est important de le dire* becomes *il est important de **ne pas** le dire*, keeping the *ne pas* together in front of the *le*.

Some other negative completers are:

ne ...jamais	never
ne ...plus	no longer
ne ...guère	hardly/scarcely
ne ...que	only
ne ...rein	nothing
ne...personne	no one

These last two have the pronouns *rien* and *personne*. They can be used as subjects too and go before the *n'/ne*:

Personne n'est arrivé	-	*No one arrived/no one has arrived*
Rien ne s'est passé	-	*Nothing happened/nothing has happened*

In these no *pas* is used!

See Chapter 5 section 1.0 for a discussion of negatives in the spoken language.

5.0 Verbs and Infinitives

In English when we use an infinitive after a verb we do not have to think; we just use the infinitive. There are a couple of exceptions such as *will, may, should, could, might, can* where we use an infinitive without *to,* for example *I may go, she will sing, they could fly* etc. However these are exceptional: most just use the standard infinitive with *to,* eg *He tries to understand, we hope to go,* etc.

In French the situation is different. There are three options. Either the infinitive is introduced by *à, de* or nothing at all, eg:

*Je commence **à** comprendre*	*I am beginning to understand*
*Elle a décidé **de** partir*	*She decided to leave*
*Je veux **[0]** dormir*	*I want to sleep*

In the last example the **[0]** just indicates that there is nothing.

There is no real system here and all you can do is to learn which verbs take which option. The lists in appendix 3 offer you a selection of the most common options. There are many more! The best thing is to pick a few and learn them and then keep expanding the stock of the ones which you know.

There are some verbs which take *de* with a following infinitive which also have an object. For example *conseiller à quelqu'un de faire - to advise someone to do.* In these examples, the person **who is being advised** is an ordinary direct object in English but in French is an indirect or *à*-phrase object. With these constructions you have to be very careful when the object of the verb is a pronoun, eg:

*Je **lui** ai conseillé de se taire*	*I advised him/her to be silent*

Because the verb *conseiller* takes an *à*-phrase object, when this is a pronoun in English such as *his/her* as in this example, you have to think carefully about which object pronoun to pick. See Chapter 3 section 2.2 on object pronouns.

6.0 Reflexive Verbs

6.1 Reflexive Pronouns

We need to consider the so-called reflexive verbs, their formation and use.

Reflexive verbs, or verbs used reflexively, have for their object one of the following non-stressable object pronouns:

me, te, se, nous, vous, se

(roughly equivalent to *myself, yourself, himself, herself, ourselves, yourselves, themselves*) and this object must agree with the subject of the verb in both person and number, giving the following pairings :

Je...me

Tu...te

Il...se

Elle...se

Nous...nous

Vous...vous

Ils...se

Elles...se

In these pronouns, *se* is only ever used reflexively whereas the others can be used as ordinary objects of a verb (see Chapter 3 section 2.2), not agreeing with the subject, for example:

Il me voit

where the *il* and the *me* do not agree.

However, *se* can only be used with third person singular or plural subjects, reflexively.

6.2 Where the pronouns go and agreement

These object pronouns when used reflexively go in the same position as when they are not used reflexively, that is directly in front of the tensed verb and in negative sentences just after the *ne*.

For example:

> *Je **me** lève*   *I (raise myself) get up* (literal meaning in brackets)
>
> *Je ne **me** lève pas*   *I don't get up*

In the *passé composé* and other compound tenses all verbs used reflexively take *être* and there is agreement of the past participle with the preceding direct object. See the section on Compound Tense Past Participle Agreement in Chapter 1 section 6.0 for fuller details.

So to give some examples:

> *Elle s'est levée*   *She (raised herself) got up*

In this example, the reflexive pronoun *s'* agrees with the subject which is feminine singular and it is the **direct** object of the verb *lever* thus making the past participle agree. However, consider the following:

> *Elle s'est envoyé une lettre*   *She sent herself a letter*

Here, the reflexive pronoun *s'* agrees with the subject which is feminine singular but this time the *s'* is the **indirect** object of the verb and so there is no agreement of the past participle. The **direct** object in this example is *une lettre*.

6.3 How reflexive structures are used

There are several ways in which reflexive verbs are used.

i)   **Genuine reflexives,** which turn back the action or process of the verb on the
            subject. Take *frapper - to hit*:

J'ai frappé la table	*I hit the table*
Je me suis frappé	*I hit myself*

In the first, the action or process of the verb carries on to *the table* and in the
second it is turned back onto *myself*. This is a very obvious physical sense of
reflexiveness, but it can be much less physical too:

Je me suis vu dans le mirroir	*I saw myself in the mirror*
Elle s'est amusée	*She amused herself (she had fun)*

ii)   **Reciprocals,** the equivalent of sentences with *each other* as the object in Eng-
            lish. These can only arise with the plural reflexives:

Nous nous aimons	*We love ourselves/each other*
Elles se connaissent	*They know each other/themselves*

As you can see there is an ambiguity in these sentences which does not exist
in English because we have the distinction between the reflexive pronouns
and the reciprocal pronoun *each other*.

iii)   Reflexives are frequently used in French where English would use a **passive**
            construction. Quite often, although not always, this is in the context of saying
            what should or should not happen or in giving instructions.

Ce vin se boit très frais	*This wine is drunk very cold*
Cela ne se fait absolument pas	*That just is not done*
La porte s'est ouverte	*The door was opened*

iv)   There are some **idiomatic** uses of reflexives and some verbs which only really exist in reflexive form. For example the verb *agir* usually means *to act* but when used reflexively it takes on the meaning of *to be a question of/to be about*:

Il s'agît de travailler très dur   *It's a question of working really hard*

S'abstenir de (to abstain from), s'accouder (to lean on one's elbows), se moquer de (to make fun of) and several others cannot be used without the reflexive pronoun and so have to be regarded as purely idiomatic from the point of view of an English speaker. You can find lists of these idiomatic reflexive verbs in most reference grammars.

v)   **Inalienable possession:** in English we say things like *He broke his leg* or *I washed my face* and so on where the *leg* and the *face* necessarily belong to the subject of the sentence. In French the possessive adjective *his* or *my* cannot be used. Instead, a reflexive construction is used:

Elle s'est cassé la jambe   (literally: *she broke to herself the leg*)

Je me suis lavé la figure   (literally: *I washed to myself the face*)

There are many other similar examples where the object affected necessarily belongs to the subject.

Of course, with the exception perhaps of the uniquely idiomatic uses above, there is really no such thing as a 'reflexive verb' because any verb which can have an object can presumably reflect the action or process of the verb back onto its subject and so make it reflexive. For example:

Elle les a accusés du vol   *She accused them of the theft*

Elle s'est accusée du vol   *She accused herself of the theft*

A little odd perhaps this last one but perfectly possible!

7.0 The Subjunctive – a starter pack

People worry about the subjunctive but there is no need to do so. The fact that we no longer have it in English should not be a problem. You do not need to 'understand' the subjunctive in order to use it correctly and successfully - you just have to learn how to form it and a few expressions which require or introduce it. After a while you begin to get a feel for it and eventually you will have a real understanding of it and why it is necessary.

Formation

Regular present tense subjunctives are formed by removing the 'ent' from the *ils/elles* form of the present tense and adding the following endings:

e	*ions*
es	*iez*
e	*ent*

These endings are the same for all three classes of verb, *-er*, *-ir* and *–re*.

For *–er* verbs, the present tense subjunctive is identical to the present indicative in all forms except the *nous* and *vous* forms. For the other two groups, the difference between indicative and subjunctive is much more marked.

There is a group of common verbs with irregular present tense subjunctive which you have to learn given below. The others you will find in any good reference grammar.

Use

The best way to go about mastering the subjunctive in practice is to learn a few common expressions which need to be followed by a verb in the subjunctive, such as:

> *Il faut que...*
>
> *Vouloir que...*
>
> *Bien que...*
>
> *Être content que...*
>
> *Il semble que...*

The first thing to notice is that the subjunctive is always preceded by an expression ending in *que* (except in set phrases such as: *Vive le Président/La Reine/la Liberté!*). This does not mean, however, that all expressions ending in *que* introduce the subjunctive.

The subjunctive is preceded by particular verbs, by *être* plus adjective, or by conjunctions. In what follows I give a jumbled assortment of ten expressions which require the subjunctive, giving a mixture of present and perfect forms, which are in practice the only tenses of the subjunctive which are used. There are, of course, many others but these will start you off.

Ten expressions taking the subjunctive:

1.	**Il faut que**	*Il faut que tu comprennes*
	It is necessary that	*You have got to understand*
2.	**Ce n'est pas que**	*Ce n'est pas que ce soit un problème difficile*
	It's not that	*It is not that it's a difficult problem*
3.	**Vouloir que**	*Je veux que tu dises la vérité*
	To wish/want that	*I want you to tell the truth*
4.	**Sans que**	*Nous l'avons vu sans qu'il le sache*
	Without	*We saw him without his knowing it*
5.	**Bien que**	*Il est fatigué bien qu'il se soit couché tôt*
	Even though	*He is tired even though he went to bed early*
6.	**Regretter que**	*Je regrette que vous ne soyez pas d'accord*
	To regret that	*I regret that you do not agree*
7.	**Pour que**	*Il a fait ça pour que tu sois content*
	So that	*He did that so that you should be happy*
8.	**Il semble que**(but not il **me** semble que)	*Il semble que vous ayez bien compris*
	It seems that	*It seems that you have understood*
9.	**Attendre que**	*J'attends que tu finisses tes devoirs*
	To wait for	*I am waiting for you to finish your homework*
10.	**When there is a superlative in the antecedent of a relative construction:**	

It is **the most beautiful picture** that I have ever seen

C'est **le plus beau tableau** que j'**aie** jamais **vu**

(perfect subjunctive, see below)

Common irregular present tense subjunctives:

Avoir	*aie, aies, ait, ayons, ayez, aient*
Être	*sois, sois, soit, soyons, soyez, soient*
Aller	*aille, ailles, aille, allions, alliez, aillent*
Faire	*fasse, fasses, fasse, fassions, fassiez, fassent*
Pouvoir	*puisse, puisses, puisse, puissions, puissiez, puissent*
Savoir	*sache, saches, sache, sachions, sachiez, sachent*
Vouloir	*veuille, veuilles, veuille, **voul**ions, **voul**iez, veuillent*

Irregular only in the *nous* and *vous* forms:

Boire	*boive, boives, boive, **buvions, buviez,** boivent*
Croire	*croie, croies, croie **croyions, croyiez,** croient*
Devoir	*doive, doives, doive, **devions, deviez,** doivent*
Prendre	*prenne, prennes, prenne, **prenions, preniez,** prennent*
Recevoir	*reçoive, reçoives, reçoive, **recevions, receviez,** reçoivent*
Tenir	*tienne, tiennes, tienne, **tenions, teniez,** tiennent*
Venir	*vienne, viennes, vienne, **venions, veniez,** viennent*
Voir	*voie, voies, voie, **voyions, voyiez,** voient*

Other subjunctive tenses

There are two other subjunctive tenses worth mentioning, the imperfect and the perfect. We will not deal with the imperfect subjunctive here because it is very rare in modern French and is dealt with very clearly in Hawkins and Towell (2015) in section 11.1.1. The perfect subjunctive is quite common and is very straightforward to form. You just use the present subjunctive of the auxiliary verbs *avoir* and *être* as appropriate along with the past participle of the verb concerned, and the rules surrounding the formation of the perfect subjunctive are exactly the same as those for the ordinary indicative tense, for example the agreement rules are the same. Here are some examples :

Even though he has finished the work ...	*Bien qu'il ait fini le travail ...*
It seems that she has returned	*Il semble qu'elle soit retournée*

Understanding the subjunctive

In most of the examples above, we are expressing something that is not agreed fact. We are expressing opinion, denial, wish, intention, emotion, regret and so on. The ordinary indicative tenses usually deal in fact and expressions of believed certainty. The subjunctive in French often adds an element of doubt or of lack of complete certainty. For example it is noted above that *il semble que...* requires the subjunctive but that *il me semble que* does not. This is because the latter is rather more what the speaker thinks, whereas the former is just an impression and so less certain. This is all very vague but if you set out by learning a selection of expressions which require the subjunctive, you will gradually gain a feeling for it and be able to use it with confidence. See Hawkins and Towell (2015) for a full treatment of the topic.

8.0 Modals

We need to say something about the verbs *devoir (must, ought to* or *to have to)*, **pouvoir** *(can* or *to be able to)* and **vouloir** *(to want)*, which are sometimes called <u>modal</u> verbs. A lot has been written about them elsewhere by other people (especially in Hawkins and Towell [2015] in sections 11.2 and 11.3) so we shall just make a few remarks here, limited to their use with infinitives and a few of their uses in some tenses.

Firstly, if they are used with another verb, they are only ever used with an infinitive form of that verb. For example:

*Je veux **partir***	*I want to leave*
*Il a pu **recommencer***	*He could/was able to start again*
*Nous devrons **finir** le travail*	*We will have to finish the work*

Secondly, the tenses of the modals are for the most part obvious as in the examples above but with *pouvoir* and *devoir* there are some difficulties. A first slight difficulty is with the word *could* which can mean either *was able to* or *would be able to*. This is easy to sort out; *was able to* becomes the perfect or imperfect tense in French, depending on whether *could/was able to* is describing an event or a state, and *would be able to* becomes the conditional. Just apply this test.

However, because the English verbs *can/could* and *must/should/ought to* are defective, not having any other form or even a real infinitive form apart from the synthetic *to be able to* or *to have to/ought to*, there are problems putting some constructions which involve them into French.

I just want to look at *must have, ought to have, should have* and *could have*. Look at the following sentences:

a)
He must have finished at 2.00	*Il a dû finir à 2.00*
They must have arrived by now	*Ils ont dû arriver avant maintenant*

b)
He ought to have written to his mother	*Il aurait dû écrire à sa mère*
They should have checked first	*Ils auraient dû contrôler d'abord*

c)
I could have seen him at 6.00	*J'aurais pu le voir à 6.00*
We could have bought that house	*Nous aurions pu acheter cette maison*

In a) we just use the perfect tense of *devoir* to express *must have* in the sense that it must be the case that something has happened. In b) and c) we use the conditional perfect tense of *devoir* and *pouvoir* respectively to express past obligation not fulfilled in b) and past possibility not fulfilled in c).

9.0 Y Avoir

You will know *il y a – there is/there are.*

You can get all tenses of this just by changing the tense of the *avoir* bit:

Present	*Il y **a***	*There is/there are*
Imperfect	*Il y **avait***	*There was/there were/there used to be*
Perfect	*Il y **a eu***	*There was (suddenly/event)*
Pluperfect	*Il y **avait eu***	*There had been*
Future	*Il y **aura***	*There will be*
Conditional	*Il y **aurait***	*There would be*
Future perfect	*Il y **aura eu***	*There will have been*
Conditional perfect	*Il y **aurait eu***	*There would have been*

Y avoir can be combined with the modal verbs *devoir* and *pouvoir* where it stays in its infinitive form:

Devoir	*Il doit **y avoir***	*There must be*
Pouvoir	*Il peut **y avoir***	*There can be*

The tenses of *devoir* and *pouvoir* can be changed:

Devoir	*Il devrait **y avoir***	*There ought to be*
Pouvoir	*Il pourrait **y avoir***	*There could be*

There is even a subjunctive of *y avoir - il y ait.* This can come after the usual subjunctive triggers such as *bien que, il faut que,* etc:

Even though there is a lot of traffic	*Bien qu'il y ait beaucoup de circulation*

If this all looks complicated, just learn the ones you might use. However, there is a system!

10.0 Conditional Structures

Conditional structures have two sections - a **condition** clause and a **consequence** clause:

> **Condition** → → → **Consequence**
>
> *If you win* → → → *I will be surprised*

Sometimes they can be the other way round and, as you see, these structures do not always involve a conditional tense. See below for the sequence of tenses.

This is the basic structure but there are strict rules governing the possible tenses used. There are three levels:

> **Present** → → → → → → **Future**
>
> *If you win* → → → → → → *I will be surprised*

> **Imperfect** → → → → → → **Conditional**
>
> *If you won/__were to win__* → → → → *I would be surprised*
>
> (Note the __were to + verb__ variant here)

> **Pluperfect** → → → → → → **Conditional perfect**
>
> *If you had won* → → → → → → *I would have been surprised*

This is the same across languages and in French, the tenses used are exactly the same:

> **Present** → → → → → → **Future**
>
> *Si tu **gagnes*** → → → → → → *je **serai** surpris*

> **Imperfect** → → → → → → **Conditional**
>
> *Si tu **gagnais*** → → → → → → *je **serais** surpris*

> **Pluperfect** → → → → → → **Conditional perfect**
>
> *Si tu **avais gagné*** → → → → → → *j'**aurais été** surpris*

So, if you understand what is going on here in English, it is a simple matter to translate these structures literally into French. You just need to analyse your English carefully.

The only complicating factor is in the use of *être* verbs, eg

> *If you had warned me, I would not have gone there*
>
> *Si tu m'avais averti, je n'y* **serais pas allé**

But you just need to think a little more carefully!

11.0 Miscellaneous constructions

11.1 Present Participles and *après avoir/être* + Past Participle

In English we use the form of the verb ending in *–ing*, sometimes known as a present participle, a great deal. The French equivalent ends in *–ant*.

However in very many cases where we use an *–ing* form in English the *-ant* form in French is impossible. The most obvious of these is in the continuous forms of English tenses (see the Tense Chart in Chapter 1 section 8.0), where the *–ing* form of the tense can only translate to the simple French version of the tense.

Contexts in which *–ant* forms can be used are the following:

i)   They can be used simply as adjectives as in the following examples where they agree in just the same way as ordinary adjectives:

a satisfying meal   *un repas satisfaisant*
an interesting story   *une histoire intéressante*

ii)   They can be used as present participles which are verbal constructions and show no agreement at all:

Talking in this way, he left the room   *Parlant ainsi, il a quitté la pièce*
Birds flying over his head woke him up   *Des oiseaux suvolant sa tête l'ont reveillé*

I found them reading letters   *Je les ai trouvés lisant des lettres*

iii)   Sometimes you can put *en* in front of the *–ant* form and this serves to emphasize the simultaneity of the process and the event and in English the word *while* is often used, as in the following:

While waiting for Godot I wrote a book   *En attendant Godot j'ai écrit un livre*
They watched the film while eating   *Ils ont regardé le film en mangeant*
I found them reading letters   *Je les ai trouvés en lisant des lettres*

In this last example the addition of *en* has a special effect. When this sentence is given without *en* in the previous set of examples, it is ambiguous as to who is reading the letters, either *I* or *they*. However, as soon as *en* is added, it can only mean that *I* was reading the letters and that *they* were found (what- or whoever they were) as a result. So be careful with this construction.

iv) A further construction in French involving the present participle can be called a compound present participle and is made up of the present participle of the auxiliary verb *avoir* or *être* with the past participle and has the force of the English construction *having done,* for example:

Having finished his work he went home *Ayant fini son travail, il est rentré*
Having arrived we opened the house *Étant arrivés nous avons ouvert la maison*

Note that when verbs requiring *être* in the compound tenses are used there is agreement with the subject of the rest of the sentence.

This construction in French also translates a fuller phrase involving the pluperfect in English, the French examples above standing just as well for the following:

When he had finished his work he went home
When we had arrived we opened the house

This is an exact equivalent to the *après avoir/être* + past participle construction below:

Ayant fini son travail, il est rentré *Après avoir fini son travail il est rentré*
Étant arrivés nous avons ouvert la maison *Après être arrivés nous avons ouvert la maison*

As you can see the agreement rules for verbs which take *être* still apply.

11.2 Il y a, venir de, être en train de, être sur le point de, depuis constructions

In this section we will look at a ragbag of constructions roughly to do with time.

11.2.1 *Il y a*

Firstly consider how to say *a period of time **ago***. This is simple. *Il y a* which we know means *there is/are* takes on this different meaning of *ago* when combined with a period of time. The formula is:

*Period of time **ago***	*Il y a period of time*
Six weeks ago	*Il y a six semaines*
Two minutes ago	*Il y a deux minutes*

This is very easy and invariable.

11.2.2 Venir de + Infinitive

This expression means *to have just done something*. In English these expressions are always either in the perfect tense or the pluperfect tense:

> *I **have** just told you...*
> *We **had** just arrived when...*

It is quite simple. The perfect tense sentences go to the present tense of *venir + de + infinitive* and the pluperfect tense sentences go to the imperfect tense of *venir + de + infinitive*, for example:

I have just told you...	*Je viens de vous dire...*
We had just arrived when...	*Nous venions d'arriver quand...*

So you just choose the correct tense of *venir* and follow this by *de* and then put the English main verb into the infinitive form rather than the past participle as in the English sentences.

He has just eaten the cake	*Il vient de manger le gateau*
They had just opened the door	*Elles venaient d'ouvrir la porte*

11.2.3 *Être en train de* + Infinitive

This is simply a construction which means *to be in the middle or process of doing*. Where in the English expression the main verb is in the present participle form, eg *He is in the middle of talking/swimming/eating* etc, in the French construction you use the appropriate form and tense of the verb *être* followed by the invariable *en train de* and then the main verb in the infinitive, eg *Il est en train de parler/nager/manger*, etc.

Here are a few examples:

They were in the middle of watching the film	*Ils étaient en train de regarder le film*
She will be in the middle of teaching	*Elle sera en train d'enseigner*

11.2.4 Être sur le point de + Infinitive

This construction means *to be about to do something*. To use this in French you simply put the verb *être* in the appropriate tense and the *sur le point de* remains invariable (apart from the *de* reducing to *d'* where necessary), eg:

They were about to eat	*Ils étaient sur le point de manger*
We are about to arrive	*Nous sommes sur le point d'arriver*
She was about to go home	*Elle était sur le point de rentrer*

11.2.5 *Depuis* construction

This construction is explained in a previous section on the Tense Chart in Chapter 1 section 8.0 but is mentioned here again for completeness.

11.2.6 Inversions

Inversion means that the subject of a sentence follows the verb instead of preceding it. There are four main contexts in which this happens:

i)   In the formation of questions when the subject is a pronoun. For example:

Vous aimez la lecture	→	*Aimez-vous la lecture ?*
You like reading	→	*Do you like reading ?*

See Chapter 2 section 3.0 on question formation.

ii)   After a piece of direct speech when saying who spoke. For example:

"Absolument pas," dit-il.   *"Absolutely not," he said.*

iii)   After words such as *peut-être (perhaps), sans doute (doubtless/without doubt)* and *à peine (hardly/scarcely)*. For example:

Peut-être l'avez-vous vue   *Perhaps you have seen her*

Sans doute sera-t-il fâché   *Doubtless he will be angry*

À peine avait-il fini son repas   *He had hardly finished his meal*

If you wish to avoid this issue quite simply do not start your sentence with these words but use the following constructions instead:

Vous l'avez peut-être vue

Il sera sans doute fâché

Il avait à peine fini son repas

With *peut-être* there is a third option of using *peut-être que* plus normal word order:

Peut-être que vous l'avez vue

iv)   In relatively formal French where inversion is necessary for the good balance of the sentence to avoid finishing it with a verb which otherwise could seem to be left dangling. After the object relative pronouns *que* and *ce que* and sometimes after the locational relative pronoun *où*, (see Chapter 3 section 3.00 for a discussion of relative pronouns) when the subject is a full noun rather than a pronoun, the verb and noun subject are inverted. For example:

Je ne sais pas ce que veut mon fils   *I do not know what my son wants*

C'est un article qu'a écrit mon père   *It is an article that my father wrote*

Voici la ville où habitent mes parents   *Here is the town where my parents live*

If you undo the inversion with some of these here you will see that they feel clumsy and unbalanced:

Je ne sais pas ce que mon fils veut

Voici la ville où mes parents habitent

They are not strictly ungrammatical like this but stylistically it is much better to invert here.

Chapter 3

Pronouns

Pronouns present a particular set of problems for native speakers of English who wish to learn French. In what follows we are going to consider the notions of subject and object and will then look at the whole range of pronouns and their behaviour in French and how to use them.

Section 1.1 concerns subjects and objects in general and is quite theoretical and at the same time quite basic so perhaps it is not for everyone. You can skip this if you feel that you are happy with the general notions of subject, direct object and indirect object and move straight to the section on French Objects, 1.2 and continue from there. However, it would be worth coming back to 1.1 at some point.

This chapter looks at subject pronouns, non-emphatic object pronouns, emphatic pronouns, relative pronouns, interrogative pronouns, demonstrative pronouns, indefinite pronouns and possessive pronouns.

1.0 Subjects and Objects

1.1 Events and Verb Types

Before we start to consider pronouns we need to consider the issue of subjects and objects in general and in French in particular.

Very generally put, language is used to talk about or describe events in the world and again, in very general terms, there are three sorts of events which can be classified as involving necessarily one, two or three things. Along with these notions of event and associated things, there are rather more peripheral elements talking about *when, where, how, why* etc the events took place, which we shall not be considering directly here.

When we talk or write about these events we use words put together in a certain way and these words correspond to the events and things associated with them. Loosely, we can equate **events** to **verbs** and the **associated things** to **subjects** and **objects**.

Events can be for example *sleeping, eating, buying, thinking, reading, dying, giving, running,* etc. The associated things or subjects and objects can be *the person sleeping, eating, buying, thinking,* etc or *the thing eaten, bought, thought, read, given,* etc.

The three sorts of event with one, two or three associated things correspond to verbs of different types:

1.1.1 Type one:

Verbs such as *sleep* or *die* are part of the first group in that they only have <u>one</u> thing associated with them:

> *He died last year*
> *They slept well*

These verbs just have a subject, the thing or person involved in the event. The other element just adds extra but not necessary information. These verbs are sometimes called intransitive verbs, meaning that they only have a subject and no object. You cannot **sleep anything** or **die anything**. This sort of verb is quite rare and is the smallest of the three groups.

1.1.2 Type two:

The vast majority of verbs fall into this category and are words such as *like, read, eat kill, understand, love* etc which have <u>two</u> things associated with them.

> *He killed the rabbit*
> *She reads the newspaper*

Each of these verbs has a subject and an object, or as is sometimes said a **do-er** and a **thing affected** by the verb. Such a definition is not always helpful or even strictly accurate but it gives a flavour of the idea of subject and object. There are other ways of defining subjects, for example, as the thing which agrees with the verb. This is not useful however in English, since there is very little agreement on verbs except for such examples as *She reads the newspaper* where the verb adds an *–s*.

However, in each example there is an event – *killing, reading* – and each event has to have two things associated with it. We call the **killer** or **reader** the subject and the

thing killed or **read** the object and in fact in English this is always called the direct object, although this only makes sense in light of the comments about indirect and direct objects below.

1.1.3 Type three:

There is a small but important group of verbs which have <u>three</u> things necessarily associated with them. They are verbs which involve the idea of transfer or transmission. The prime example of these verbs is *give*. With this type of verb there is **a source, a goal** and **a thing or idea transferred** between the two. For example:

> *She gave John the bag/she gave the bag to John*

In this sentence, *She* is the **source**, *John/to John* is the **goal** and *the bag* is the **thing transferred**. As you can see from the next two examples, the **thing transferred** does not have to be physical but can be **an idea**.

> *He told them a joke/He told a joke to them*
> *We read you the story/We read the story to you*

In English grammar, the **thing or idea transferred** is the direct object and the **goal** is the indirect object. They can almost always exist in the two different versions shown above where *John, them* and *you* can go after the direct object in a **to-phrase**: *to John, to them* and *to you*. This can be used as a test in English to see if an object is indirect.

The objects of verbs in type two above are always considered to be direct objects, perhaps because they are usually in some sense directly affected by the action of the verb rather than in the sense identified here where there is a contrast between direct and indirect objects with these transfer verbs. So in English, if a verb only has one object then it is always considered to be a direct object. This is not the case in French.

1.2 Objects in French

In French the situation is very similar, although importantly different in a particular way. In English, indirect objects can be expressed as a **to-phrase** and placed after the direct object. In French almost all indirect objects, with the exception of a group of pronouns which we will deal with in detail below, must be in the French equivalent of the **to-phrase**, namely the **à-phrase**. They do not have the equivalent of the other English option in front of the direct object without the *à*. So the French equivalent of *She gave John the bag/she gave the bag to John* can only be

> *Elle a donné le sac à Jean*

We will look at the other examples involving the pronouns *them* and *you* in depth below.

The other difference is that mentioned above, where a verb which we in English would consider to have a direct object because it only has one object has an indirect object introduced by *à* in French, for example *to please* in English has only one object which is therefore a direct object. However, the French equivalent *plaire* must have an object introduced by *à*, thus making the object indirect in French:

> *That pleases his mother*
> *Cela plait **à sa mère***

This is an important difference between the two languages and the verbs which behave like this simply have to be learned.

In general it is fair to say that an indirect object in French is one which, when involving a full noun, is introduced by *à*. So looking at indirect objects entirely within the French language and not in relation to English, we can treat this as a definition.

2.0 Pronouns in French

2.1 Subject pronouns (weak, non-emphatic or non-stressable)

These pronouns determine the agreement of the verb and are the familiar *je, tu, il, elle, on, nous, vous, ils, elles*. They are not stressable and must always be in front of the verb that agrees with them:

> *Je connais ces filles*
> *Vous avez vu mon oncle*

There is nothing particularly remarkable about them except that they cannot be joined with full nouns or with other pronouns as their equivalents in English can, in structures such as:

> *John and I, you and Lucy, he and I, etc*

In these contexts you have to use a different set of stressable pronouns which we will look at later. See Chapter 3 section 2.3.

2.2 Object pronouns (weak, non-emphatic or non-stressable)

In English these are words like *me, her, us, him, them*, etc which cannot be the subject of the verb.

When translating into French there is not a simple one-to-one correlation between the English object pronouns and the French ones. The following table shows the correspondence:

English to French Object Pronoun Correspondence							
	me	you	him	her	it	us	you	them
Direct object	*me*	*te*	*le*	*la*	*le/la*	*nous*	*vous*	*les*
Indirect object	*me*	*te*	*lui*	*lui*	*lui*	*nous*	*vous*	*leur*

From this you can see that there is no problem in choosing the right French equivalent for *me, you* (singular), *us* and *you* (plural) where the correspondence is one-to-one. The only difficulties arise in the third person pronouns, *him, her, it* and *them*. English makes no distinction in the form of the word between direct and indirect object pronouns, so *me, him, you, them*, etc can do both jobs. The same is true for the first and second person singular and plural object pronouns in French and so we do not have to think when choosing them. The difficult decision to be made is whether the third person object pronouns in English should be the direct or indirect objects in French and we cannot tell this by looking at the form of the English pronoun. So this is where our understanding of the notion of direct and indirect objects is very important. There is also a small problem concerning gender in the third person singular pronouns where, as you can see, the French pronoun *lui* can mean either *him* or *her*.

These French pronouns can be looked at in a different way in the following table, along with *y* and *en* which we will explain later.

Order and Nature of French Object Pronouns				
Column 1	Column 2	Column 3	Column 4	Column 5
Direct/ Indirect	Direct	Indirect replaces human *à*-phrases	Replaces *à/dans* phrases (non-human)	Replaces *de* phrases
me				
te	*le*			
[se]	*la*	*lui*	*y*	*en*
nous	*les*	*leur*		
vous				

In this table, column 1 contains pronouns which can be either direct objects or indirect objects. They are also the reflexive pronouns, including *se*. Column 2 contains third person direct objects and column 3 contains third person indirect objects when they are human. *Y* stands for phrases introduced by *à* or *dans* when they are non-human, and *en* stands for phrases introduced by *de*.

This table is extremely important because it gives the order of pronouns when two are needed together. The order is left to right following the arrows.

We will first of all look at the positioning of these object pronouns and then go on to deal with the question of making the correct choice of pronoun and then complete this section on non-stressable pronouns by considering pronoun order when two or more are needed.

2.2.1 Position of the object pronouns

All pronouns in this section are weak and non-stressable and are always found in a 'protected' position in front of the verb or verbs of which they are object. In English object pronouns go in exactly the same position the nouns they replace, but in French this is not the case.

*She reads **the book***	*Elle lit **le livre***
*She reads **it***	*Elle **le** lit*

This is a very important difference between the two languages. In the compound tenses, the pronoun has to go in front of the auxiliary verb as well:

They saw the horses	*Ils ont vu les chevaux*
They saw them	*Ils **les** ont vus*

In a negative sentence the pronoun comes after the *ne* but before the verb or verbs:

She does not read the book	*Elle ne lit pas le livre*
She does not read it	*Elle ne **le** lit pas*
They did not see the horses	*Ils n'ont pas vu les chevaux*
They did not see them	*Ils ne **les** ont pas vus*

We need to say a few words about pronoun position in imperatives (see also Chapter 2 section 2.0). Normally, when not using an imperative, object pronouns such as *le, la* and *les* have to go in front of the verb as discussed, as in *Je la vois – I see her*. However in positive commands in French this is the only time when the object pronouns will come after the verb, for example:

Eat it!	*Mange-le!*
Catch her!	*Attrape-la!*

Also in these positive commands, the non-stressable object pronouns *me* and *te* are replaced by their stressable equivalents *moi* and *toi* (see Chapter 3 section 2.3 for full details of these stressable pronouns), for example:

Give me the book   *Donnez-moi le livre*

As you can see too, all of these pronouns which come after the verb in positive commands are linked to the verb by a hyphen.

In negative commands the pronouns go in their usual position in front of the verb, and we use the usual non-stressable versions, for example:

Don't give me the book   *Ne me donnez pas le livre*
Don't eat it   *Ne le mange pas*
Don't catch her   *Ne l'attrape pas*

2.2.2 Choosing the correct pronoun

First and second person objects

The pronouns in column 1 are the easiest to deal with and leaving out *se* for the moment (we will deal with reflexive pronouns separately - see Chapter 2 section 6.0) are the direct equivalents of *me, you* (singular), *us* and *you* (plural). Consider these examples:

He sends me flowers   *Il m'envoie des fleurs*
John will see me tomorrow   *Jean me verra demain*
I hate you   *Je te déteste*
She will speak to you soon   *Elle te parlera bientôt*
He spoke to us   *Il nous a parlé*
My father prefers us   *Mon père nous préfère*
I see you   *Je vous vois*
They spoke to you yesterday   *Ils vous ont parlé hier*

As you see, this is easy. All you have to remember is that when the pronoun in English is preceded by *to* you must not have the equivalent of *to* in French but just use the pronoun in front of the verb. Also, you can see that for reasons of pronunciation, *me* and *te* must reduce to *m'* and *t'* in front of a word beginning with a vowel.

Third person objects

We now come on to the third person object pronouns in columns 2 and 3. Here we are faced with two problems; firstly we must decide when the English pronouns *him, her, it* and *them* translate to their direct or indirect object equivalents (and our discussion of direct and indirect pronouns and the nature of French indirect object pronouns in Chapter 3 section 1.2 is very important here); secondly, as already mentioned, we need to be aware that both *him* and *her* can translate to *lui*. This is not a real problem but just needs some level of awareness. For ease of reference we will repeat the pronoun order chart here:

Order and Nature of French Object Pronouns				
Column 1	Column 2	Column 3	Column 4	Column 5
Direct/ Indirect	Direct	Indirect replaces human *à*-phrases	Replaces *à/dans* phrases (non-human)	Replaces *de* phrases
me				
te	*le*			
[se]	*la*	*lui*	*y*	*en*
nous	*les*	*leur*		
vous				

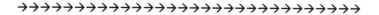

Let us now look at some examples:

They saw her in the town   *Ils l'ont vue à la ville*

Here *her* translates to *la* which becomes *l'* for reasons of pronunciation. This is the direct object of the verb *voir* and so the pronoun is chosen from column 2 and can show the correct gender. Note too that there is preceding direct object agreement.

We know her   *Nous la connaissons*

Here *her* translates to *la*. This is the direct object of the verb *connaître* and so the pronoun is chosen from column 2 and can show the correct gender, without having to reduce to *l'*.

I sent him the money   *Je lui ai envoyé l'argent*

In this example, *him* translates to *lui* because the person or thing to which something is sent is the indirect or *à*-object in French. Additionally here the indirect object is human and so the pronoun is chosen from column 3 and is the singular pronoun *lui*. The pronoun *lui* can be either masculine or feminine but it is usually very clear from the context.

I hate him   *Je le déteste*

Here *him* translates to *le* because the verb *détester* has a direct noun object, not an *à*-object, and so the pronoun is chosen from column 2 and shows the gender.

I told her the story   *Je lui ai raconté l'histoire*

In this example *her* translates to *lui* because the person or thing to which something is told is the indirect or *à*-object in French. Again the indirect object here is human and so the pronoun is chosen from column 3. *Lui* is used but here it is feminine, although you cannot tell this from its form, but again the context makes it clear.

I met them yesterday   *Je les ai rencontrés hier*

Here *them* translates to *les* because the verb *rencontrer* has a direct noun object and not an *à*-phrase object and so the plural pronoun is chosen from column 2.

He gave them the advice   *Il leur a donné le conseil*

In this example, *them* translates to *leur* because the person or thing to which something is given is the indirect or *à*-object in French and the plural pronoun is chosen from column 3.

We must turn now to columns 4 and 5, involving *y* and *en*. It is difficult to talk about these two pronouns in terms of translating them from specific English words or phrases. *Y* often translates the English adverb *there* as in *he goes there – il y va*. However, this is not always the case. The same sort of thing is true for *en*, which often but not always translates *of it/them* as in *I am proud of it – J'en suis fier*. Instead of approaching these words from English, it will be better to look at their behaviour just within French.

Y

Let us look at *y* first of all. As it says at the top of column 4, *y* replaces *à* or *dans* phrases when they are non-human. So any verb or adjective which requires an *à* or *dans* phrase after it could have it replaced by *y* if it involves a non-human noun. Let us consider some examples:

*Elle est allée **à Bruges***	*Elle **y** est allée*
She went to Bruges	*She went there*

Aller requires an *à* object after it and so it is replaced quite naturally by *y*, which in this case has the very common translation into English of *there*.

*Mon frère est entré **dans le bâtiment***	*Mon frère **y** est entré*
My brother entered the building	*My brother entered it*

In English *enter* just has a direct object but in French *entrer* used in this way must have the preposition *dans* before the place entered. So here there is no real translation in English of *y*.

*Je pensais **à mes vacances***	*J'**y** pensais*
I was thinking about my holidays	*I was thinking about them*

In French *penser* needs an *à*-phrase after it when the meaning is *to consider something* and this quite naturally reduces to *y*.

*Elle était prête **à se mettre en route***	*Elle **y** était prête*
She was ready to set off	*She was ready to do it*

This is a bit of an awkward translation but it expresses the meaning in this context. (*She was ready to do it* can also be translated by *Elle était prête à le faire*.) The adjective *prêt/prête* requires an *à* object after it which in both examples here involves an infinitive.

Je m'étais décidé **à travailler dur**	*Je m'**y** étais décidé*
I had made up my mind to work hard	*I had made up my mind to do it*

Again this is a slightly awkward translation but it gives the meaning contained within *y* in the example. (*I had made up my mind to do it* can also be translated by *Je m'étais décidé à le faire.*) *Se décider* requires *à* before its dependent infinitive.

Il hésitait **à l'interrompre**	*Il **y** hésitait*
He hesitated to interrupt him	*He hesitated to do it*

Yet again, the translation is slightly awkward but it captures the meaning. *Hésiter* requires *à* before a following infinitive.

There is a variety of possible translations of *y* into English as the examples above show but what is clear is that within French, *y* behaves in a thoroughly predictable fashion, being the pronoun (or in fact, technically, the pro-prepositional phrase) for the French prepositional phrases introduced by *à* and *dans* which contain non-human nouns or even infinitives.

En

In a very similar way, *en* is the pronoun (or as we might call it the pro-prepositional phrase) for prepositional phrases introduced by *de*. Again, it is difficult to provide a single translation for the word *en*. Often but not always as you will see below, it will translate to *of it/them*. Any verb, noun or adjective which requires a *de* phrase after it could have it replaced by *en*. Let us consider some examples:

J'ai peur **des chiens**	*J'**en** ai peur*
I am afraid of dogs	*I am afraid of them*

Avoir peur has to have a *de* object which will change to *en* when it needs to become a pronoun.

Je suis fier **de ta réussite**	*J'**en** suis fier*
I am proud of your success	*I am proud of it*

Fier de means *proud of* and the *de* phrase converts to *en* when it needs to become a pronoun.

Elle avait besoin **d'un stylo**	*Elle **en** avait besoin*
She needed a pen	*She needed it*

Just like *avoir peur, avoir besoin* has to have a *de* object and so behaves in the same way.

*Nous sommes contents **du résultat***	*Nous **en** sommes contents*
We are happy with the result	*We are happy with it*

Content like the adjective *fier* needs a *de* after it and behaves in the same way.

*J'ai **des pommes***	*J'**en** ai*
I have some apples	*I have some*

Here we have the partitive *de,* expressing quantity and roughly meaning *some.* It behaves in just the same way as any other *de* expression.

*Il prend **du poulet***	*Il **en** prend*
He takes some chicken	*He takes some*

Again this is an example of the partitive *de* meaning roughly *some* and it behaves in the same way.

*Il a parlé **du voyage***	*Il **en** a parlé*
He talked about the journey	*He talked about it*

Here *parler* requires a *de* object which converts to *en* when it needs to become a pronoun.

*Nous les avons remerciés **de leur aide***	*Nous les **en** avons remerciés*
We thanked them for their help	*We thanked them for it*

Again, *remercier* requires a *de* object for the thing for which thanks is being given. As expected this *de* object converts to *en* when necessary.

In this last example we have the two object pronouns *les* and *en* appearing together and in the next section we need to discuss how we choose the correct order in these circumstances.

2.2.3 Choosing the right pronoun order

For ease of reference we repeat the pronoun table yet again here:

Order and Nature of French Object Pronouns				
Column 1	Column 2	Column 3	Column 4	Column 5
Direct/ Indirect	Direct	Indirect replaces human *à*-phrases	Replaces *à/dans* phrases (non-human)	Replaces *de* phrases
me				
te	*le*			
[se]	*la*	*lui*	*y*	*en*
nous	*les*	*leur*		
vous				
1	2	3	4	5

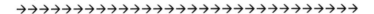

When two or more of these pronouns appear together as objects of the same construction, we need to be able to put them in the correct order. This is very easy. Once we have chosen correctly which pronouns are needed, it is a simple matter of picking them from the above table, following the direction of the arrows underneath.

Let us look at some examples.

> *He gave them it*   *Il le leur a donné*

Here we have decided that *it* is the direct object referring to a masculine thing and that *them*, as discussed above, is the indirect object. These will translate to the French pronouns *le* and *leur* respectively. Following the direction of the arrows from left to right we first pick *le* from column 2 and then *leur* from column 3, keeping them in that order, and place them both in front of the whole of the verb, in this example, *a donné*.

> *She sent them to us*   *Elle nous les a envoyé(e)s*

In this example, *them* is the plural direct object and the phrase *to us* is the indirect object which will translate to *les* and *nous* respectively. Again, following the direction of the arrows from left to right we first pick *nous* from column 1 and then *les* from column 2. Again preserving that order we place them in front of the verb *a envoyé(e)s*.

> *They saw me there*   *Ils m'y ont vu*

In this example, *me* is the direct object and *there* is translated here by *y*. So from left to right in the table we pick *me* first and then *y*. *Me* reduces to *m'* in front of the vowel-like *y*, giving the expected result.

> *He gave me some*   *Il m'en a donné*

Here in English, *me* is the indirect object and *some* is the direct object. For the English pronoun *me* we pick the French pronoun *me*. However, for the English pronoun *some*, we have to choose *en*, because in French this is the partitive construction involving *de* in the original full version of the sentence, as shown in the immediately preceding section. So, *me* reduces to *m'* in front of *en*, giving the correct translation, following the order in the table.

> *He told her it there*   *Il le lui y a raconté*

In this example, which is a bit odd but possible, *her* is the indirect object, *it* is the direct object and *there* is a location expression. From the table we select *le* from column 2, *lui* from column 3 and *y*, the usual translation for *there* from column 4.

From these examples we can see that there is not a fixed order of, say, direct followed by indirect objects; rather the order is strictly determined by the order of columns 1 to 5 in the table.

2.3 Emphatic, strong or stressable pronouns

So far we have considered only the weak or non-emphatic pronouns which are restricted in terms of their position to a protected slot in front of the verb. There is another set of pronouns which can take stress and which are used in different positions and contexts. Here is the set of emphatic (also called strong or stressable) pronouns:

Emphatic Pronouns	
Moi	*Nous*
Toi	*Vous*
Lui	*Eux*
Elle	*Elles*

We should point out that there is a gender distinction in the third person pronouns in both singular and plural. *Lui* in this context is masculine and is equivalent only to *him* or *it* when it refers to a masculine item. This contrasts with *lui* in the non-stressable pronouns which can be either masculine or feminine. *Eux* is masculine third person plural, meaning *them* when it is masculine plural or mixed (masculine and feminine) plural. There is of course some overlap with the non-stressable pronouns in the *nous* and *vous* form.

2.3.1 After prepositions

Emphatic pronouns are used in contexts where they can bear stress. One such context is after prepositions. Consider the following examples:

for me	*pour moi*
with them	*avec eux/elles*
after him	*après lui*
without her	*sans elle*
in front of you	*derrière toi*
mine	*à moi* (possessive pronoun for use with *être* - see Chapter 3 section 7.0)

These pronouns must be used in this context because they can bear stress. Non-emphatic pronouns just cannot work here.

2.3.2 Positive commands

Another context where these pronouns have to be used has already been mentioned (see Chapter 2 section 2.0) which is positive commands where the object is first or second person singular. We repeat the example here for clarity:

Give me the book *Donnez-moi le livre*

In the negative, this reverts to the usual non-stressable pronoun in front of the verb:

Do not give me the book *Ne me donnez pas le livre*

2.3.3 Emphasis

Naturally, emphatic pronouns are used to highlight individuals in a sentence. Sometimes these pronouns can have -*même* suffixed to them for extra emphasis. For example:

Me? I have no idea. What about you? *Moi? Je n'ai aucune idée. Et toi ?*
***He** knows nothing* *Lui, il n'en sait rien*
It was me who finished first *C'était moi qui ai fini le premier*
He finished it himself *Il l'a fini lui-même*

2.3.4 Comparison

These pronouns are used when pronouns appear in comparison sentences:

He is younger than I/me *Il est plus jeune que moi*
She is taller than he/him *Elle est plus grande que lui*

2.3.5 Conjoined structures

If either element of a conjoined structure is a pronoun then it has to be one of the stressable pronouns:

My father and I arrived at six *Mon père et moi sommes arrivés à six*
He and I played cards together *Lui et moi avons joué ensemble aux cartes*

In short if one of these types of pronoun has to appear in any position other than the protected position just in front of the verb, it has to be one of these stressable or emphatic pronouns.

3.0 Relative pronouns

First of all we need to consider relative pronouns and structures in English and discuss what they in fact are. Relative structures are used to provide information about or a definition of something, for example *she is a woman who lives in Brighton*. Here we are talking about *a woman* and giving a little more information about her in the part of the sentence after the relative pronoun *who*, which "relates" the *woman* to the extra information.

As just shown, in English relative pronouns are words like *which, that, who, (whom)*. And sometimes in English we can miss them out altogether without changing the meaning. The sorts of sentence which have relative pronouns are:

1   This is <u>the book</u> **(which)** I bought
2   He is <u>the man</u> **who** eats snakes
3   This is <u>the jumper</u> **(that)** I want
4   I have seen <u>the person</u> **(who/whom)** you called

There are several things we need to talk about here.

There is a general structure common to them all where three things are important. There is a **noun phrase,** which can also be known as the **antecedent**, which is underlined and a **relative pronoun**, which is in bold. Some of these relative pronouns are in brackets and this is to show that they can be missed out in English and the sentence will still mean the same. Finally there is a **section of sentence** containing at least a verb following the relative pronoun. You can write a formula which captures this:

[Noun Phrase] (Relative Pronoun) [Sentence]

What a relative pronoun does is to link the noun phrase or antecedent either to the subject or the object role of the verb in the sentence which follows. So, in *1* above, *the book* works as the object of *bought*. In *2*, *the man* works as the subject of *eats*, and so on.

Being able to understand and sort out the idea of linking the noun phrase to subject or object role in the following sentence is the key to understanding how to get these right in French.

One test to see if you have an object relative is to establish whether you can miss out the relative pronoun. So in *1, 3* and *4* above the relative pronouns are all object relatives because they can be missed out in English.

Another test is to look at the common sense meaning of the sentence and to look at whether the verb has a subject already or perhaps an object already. If one of those roles is used up then you cannot be linking to that role.

3.1 Basic relative structures in French

In French, as usual, the situation is different. Firstly, you can never leave a relative pronoun out. It is just plain wrong if you do. Secondly, it really matters which relative pronoun you use. In all four of the examples in English above, you could just use *that*. There is not this freedom in French.

The basic French relative pronouns are *qui* and *que; qui* is the subject relative pronoun and *que* is the object relative pronoun. So what this means is that *que* would be used in the equivalent of *1, 3* and *4* above and *qui* would be used for *2*:

1	*C'est le livre* **que** *j'ai acheté*
2	*C'est l'homme* **qui** *mange des serpents*
3	*Celui-ci est le pullover* **que** *je veux*
4	*J'ai vu la personne* **que** *tu as appelée*

These words must be there. French shares the same general structure with English relative sentences but has the restriction that the relative pronoun must be there.

There are times, however, when the relative pronoun refers to the whole of the preceding idea and not just the nearest noun phrase in the antecedent. Consider the following sentence:

She bought that book which was interesting

It is ambiguous between whether it was *the book* which *was interesting* (meaning 1) or *the fact that she had bought it* which *was interesting* (meaning 2). In French this ambiguity does not exist because you use a slightly different relative pronoun to distinguish the meanings. Meaning 1 is expressed by the ordinary relative pronoun and meaning 2 by the relative pronoun *ce qui/ce que*. Here are the translations with the antecedent in square brackets:

> 1   *Elle a acheté [ce livre]* **qui** *est intéressant*
>
> 2   *[Elle a acheté ce livre]* **ce qui** *est intéressant*

There is another use of *ce qui/ce que* where it has the force of *what* in English in the following context:

> *What I prefer is...*   *Ce que je préfère c'est....*
>
> *What interests me is...*   *Ce qui m'intéresse c'est....*

In the first example, *what* is the object of *prefer* and so is *ce que* and in the second, *what* is the subject of *interests* and so is *ce qui*.

Another relative pronoun to consider is the locational relative pronoun *où*. This is the equivalent of *in which* or *where* used in the following contexts:

> *The house which she lived in*   *La maison où elle habitait*
>
> *The shop where he buys his clothes*   *Le magasin où il achète ses*
>   *vêtements*

Où is always preferred in these constructions to the more complex preposition + *lequel* which might seem to be the answer (see the end of section 3.2 below).

3.2 More complex relatives in French

So far we have only looked at the basic relative pronouns *qui/que* and *ce qui/ce que*. There are others which we need to consider here. These further options involve relative constructions where there is a preposition. In English if we have a relative construction which includes a preposition we usually leave it dangling at the end of the sentence. Here are some examples:

> *It is something which I cannot understand the importance **of***
> *She is the lady who I sent the letter **to***
> *It was that concert which she took part **in***

This just is not possible in French. In fact more old-fashioned speakers of English find this form unacceptable and would prefer the following:

> *It is something **of** which I cannot understand the importance*
> *She is the lady **to** who(m) I sent the letter*
> *It was that concert **in** which she took part*

This is the exact parallel of the structure which has to be used in French. There are three ways of doing this with various prepositions in French.

Firstly, there is the word *dont* which means roughly *whose/of whom/of which*. Just as *en* replaces *de*-phrases in ordinary pronoun object structures in front of the verb, *dont* deals with *de*-phrases when they are involved in relative structures:

> *It is something **of** which I cannot understand the importance*
> *C'est quelque chose **dont** je ne comprends pas l'importance*

Any structure which requires *de* after it will involve *dont* in a relative clause. So you have to be aware which structures use *de* in French because they will often end up looking very different from their English equivalents which do not always have *of*, such as in the *need/avoir besoin de* example here:

> *Something which I really need*   *Quelque chose **dont** j'ai vraiment besoin*
> *Someone I am very proud of*   *Quelqu'un **dont** je suis très fier*

Secondly, when the antecedent is human or animate, you use just the same strategy as old-fashioned speakers of English do. You put the preposition in front of the relative pronoun *qui* in the position just after the antecedent. For example:

The man who I work for	*L'homme **pour qui** je travaille*
The friend that I went to the opera with	*L'ami **avec qui** je suis allé à l'opéra*
The teacher I sent the letter to	*Le prof **à qui** j'ai envoyé la lettre*

Thirdly in the sort of structure where the antecedent is not human or animate, we do not use *qui* but a special relative pronoun *lequel* which has four forms according to the gender and number of the antecedent. It is also an interrogative pronoun (see immediately below):

Interrogative Pronouns		
	Singular	Plural
Masculine	*lequel*	*lesquels*
Feminine	*laquelle*	*lesquelles*

Consider the following examples:

The table on which he was working	*La table sur laquelle il travaillait*
The cards which they were playing with	*Les cartes avec lesquelles ils jouaient*
The concert after which they ate	*Le concert après lequel ils ont mangé*

Because the antecedent is non-human we do not use *qui* but select the correct form of *lequel*, according to the table above.

4.0 Interrogative pronouns

There are two main interrogative pronouns, *qui/que* and *lequel* and they are fairly straightforward.   These pronouns are used in questions and mean *who/which* and *which one(s)* respectively. In this context *qui* is used exclusively for humans and refers to both subjects and objects, *que* is used exclusively for non-humans and it is used only for object questions in normal inversion questions structures. It appears in the *Qu'est-ce que/qui* form of question formation for both subject and object questions. *Lequel* with the same masculine/feminine/singular/plural variants as in section 3.2 above is used for both humans and non-humans and it too is used for both subjects and objects. Consider these examples:

Who (has) arrived?	*Qui est arrivé?*
Who did you see?	*Qui as-tu vu?*
What did you want?	*Que voulais-tu?*
What happened?	*Qu'est-ce qui est arrivé*
Which ones (fem) do you want?	*Lesquelles préfères-tu?*
Which one (masc) *is better?*	*Lequel est meilleur?*

5.0 Demonstrative pronouns

Demonstrative pronouns in English are the words *this (one), that (one), these (ones) those (ones)* and are expressed in French using the following:

Demonstrative Pronouns		
	Singular	Plural
Masculine	*celui*	*ceux*
Feminine	*celle*	*celles*

In the singular *celui* and *celle* both mean *this* and *that* depending on gender and *ceux* and *celles* both mean *these* and *those* depending on gender too.   Context generally makes it clear which is meant but if it is necessary to make it even clearer then we can add the suffix *–ci* showing that it is either *this* or *these,*or the suffix *–là* showing that it is either *these* or *those*. Here are some examples:

Where are my books? These are not the right ones.
Où sont mes livres? Ceux-ci ne sont pas les bons.

Use this door. That one is locked.
Utilisez cette porte. Celle-là est fermée à clef.

Of all the poems this one is the best
De tous les poèmes celui-ci est le meilleur

6.0 Indefinite pronouns

There is a group of pronouns which can be used when not referring to an entity or concept with a specific gender. *Cela, ça* both mean *that*, with *ça* being the more informal of the two and more likely to be used in speech. *Ceci* means *this*. They can be used either as subjects or objects of verbs and can come after prepositions. You use them if you wish not to make reference to a specific noun but rather to a general situation. For example:

Getting up early! I don't like that	*Se/me lever tôt, je n'aime pas cela/ça*
Anything else? (in a shop)	*Et avec ceci?*
That's not funny	*Ça n'est pas drôle*
It lasts a long time	*Ça dure longtemps*
Cheating! I cannot stand that	*Tricher! Je ne supporte pas cela/ça*

7.0 Possessive pronouns

Possessive pronouns in English are the following

mine, yours, his, hers, its, ours, yours, theirs

and can stand alone as subjects or objects of verbs or after prepositions. For example:

*Your cooking was good but **mine** was better*
*Of the two books **his** was the more interesting*

We should point out here the difference between the possessive pronouns which we are dealing with here and the possessive articles (see Chapter 4 section 3.3). The possessive articles are the words

my, your, his, her, its, our, your, their

and cannot stand alone but must be with a noun as in *my brother* or *her friend*. We will leave these here and just note that they exist and deal with them in the adjective section.

In French the possessive pronouns are the following:

Possessive Pronouns						
	First person singular mine	Second person singular yours	Third person singular his/hers/its	First person plural ours	Second person plural yours	Third person plural theirs
Masculine Singular	*le mien*	*le tien*	*le sien*	*le nôtre*	*le vôtre*	*le leur*
Feminine Singular	*la mienne*	*la tienne*	*la sienne*	*la nôtre*	*la vôtre*	*la leur*
Masculine Plural	*les miens*	*les tiens*	*les siens*	*les nôtres*	*les vôtres*	*les leurs*
Feminine Plural	*les miennes*	*les tiennes*	*les siennes*	*les nôtres*	*les vôtres*	*les leurs*

This looks complicated but it is not. All you have to do is to remember that as usual you choose the pronoun based on the gender and number of the noun for which it is standing. The only odd thing for speakers of English is that we differentiate the gender of the owner or possessor in the third person. So we have *his, hers* and *its*. In French this does not happen and so the pronouns from the third person singular column in the table all mean *his, hers* and *its*, the pronoun, as usual, being chosen on the basis of the gender and number of the noun to which it refers.

Here again are the two example English sentences now with their French equivalents:

> *Your cooking was good but **mine** was better*
> *Ta cuisine était bonne mais **la mienne** était meilleure*

In this example, *cuisine* is feminine and singular and the possessor is first person singular and so we choose *la mienne* from the table.

> *Of the two books **his** was more interesting*
> *Des deux livres le sien était plus intéressant*

In this example *livres* is masculine plural but the pronoun when used is masculine singular because we are only talking about one of the books. The possessor is third person singular and so we choose *le sien* from the table. If the sentence were *of the two books **hers** was more interesting* it would still have the same translations *des deux livres le sien était plus intéressant* because the gender of the pronoun is determined by the noun which it stands for. The difference between the two is worked out from the context because no pronoun is used in a vacuum. All pronouns are used as a short-hand in a context where all parties involved are aware of the people and things being referred to.

There is one case which we have not mentioned. With the verb *être* we tend not to use these standard possessive pronouns but rather we use the preposition *à* with the appropriate emphatic pronoun:

> *It is mine*   *C'est à moi*
> *This book is hers*   *Ce livre est à elle*
> *Is this car yours?*   *Est-ce que cette voiture est à vous/toi ?*

Chapter 4

Adjectives, Adverbs and Articles

1.0 Adjectives

There are three specific issues which the English-speaking learner of French has to consider when dealing with ordinary adjectives. These are position, agreement and comparison and are the principal areas where the two languages deal with adjectives differently. We will look at these in turn, and then at the behaviour of adjectives with a following infinitive or clause.

1.1 Position

Quite simply adjectives in English come before the noun which they describe in a noun phrase. There are some quite complicated rules about the ordering of adjectives by type when two or more are used together but we do not need to worry about them. The other option is that they come after verbs such as *to be, to seem, to become* etc. Here are some examples of both type of usage:

The **incompetent** teacher	A **happy** woman	An **old** car
The teacher was **incompetent**	The woman seems **happy**	The car is **old**

In French, the situation is a little different. Although the use after the equivalents of the verbs *to be, to become, to seem* etc is pretty much the same, the positioning of adjectives which describe nouns is rather different.

These English examples become the following in French:

*Le prof **incompétent***	*Une femme **heureuse***	*Une **vieille** voiture*
*Le prof était **incompétent***	*La femme semble **heureuse***	*La voiture est **vieille**.*

Most adjectives come after the noun in French. However, there is a group of fairly common adjectives which usually come before the noun. The most common are the following:

beau	*handsome/beautiful*
bon	*good*
joli	*pretty*
mauvais	*bad*
nouveau	*new*
petit	*small*
vieux	*old*

There are more and these can be found in good reference grammars such as Hawkins and Towell (2015).

Look at the following:

an **interesting** story	*une histoire **intéressante***
a **small** boy	*un **petit** garçon*
a **new** house	*une **nouvelle** maison*
a **yellow** parrot	*un perroquet **jaune***

In these we have examples of those which come before the noun as well as those which come after the noun. You just have to learn which ones go where.

There are some other issues surrounding the position of adjectives. Some change their meaning depending on whether they come before or after the noun. Two common examples are *ancien* and *propre*. When it comes in front of the noun, *ancien* means *former*. When it comes after the noun, it means *ancient/old*. With *propre*, when it comes before the noun it means *own* and after the noun it means *clean*. Here are some examples:

my own room	*ma propre chambre*
my clean room	*ma chambre propre*
an ancient/old teacher	*un prof ancien*
a former teacher	*un ancien prof*

There are others and you just have to learn them as you come across them. See Hawkins and Towell (2015) or any other good reference grammar for a full list.

1.2 Agreement

This is an issue which we just do not have in English. An adjective is just an adjective and we use it without altering its form. However, in French adjectives agree with the noun or nouns which they describe in both gender and number.

Let us use the French adjective *grand* as an example. To mark masculine we add nothing, to mark feminine agreement we add *−e* and to mark plural agreement we add *−s* so *grand* changes as in the following table:

Regular Adjective Agreement		
	Singular	Plural
Masculine	*grand*	*grands*
Feminine	*grande*	*grandes*

Here are some examples:

a big chair	*une grande chaise*
seven big men	*sept grands hommes*
the big tables	*les grandes tables*
a big man	*un grand homme*

This then is the basic system of adjectival agreement. There are of course exceptions to this basic method where because of the spelling we cannot follow these rules and we will consider some of them now.

If an adjective naturally ends in an *−e* such as *facile* we do not add an extra *−e* in the feminine singular.

If an adjective naturally ends in *−s* such as *bas* we do not add an extra *−s* in the masculine plural.

Apart from this there are groups of exceptions which serve to reflect change in pronunciation in feminine forms such as doubling of consonants or use of a grave accent such as *gras/grasse(s)* – *fat* or *complet/complète(s)* – *full/complete*. As well as this there are other regular alterations for adjectives with particular endings in the masculine which change in the feminine:

-eux/-euse	*heureux/heureuse*	*happy*
-eau/-elle	*beau/belle*	*beautiful*
-f/-ve	*actif/active*	*active*

And there are some consistent irregularities in the formation of plurals. A lot (but not all) of adjectives ending in *–al* form their masculine plural in *–aux* and adjectives ending in *–eau* generally form their masculine plural by adding *-x* . Here are some examples:

général/généraux	*general*
nouveau/nouveaux	*new*

For complete lists of these irregularities please consult a good reference grammar such as Hawkins and Towell (2015) or Bryne and Churchill (1993).

Adjectives such as *beau* and *nouveau* have a special masculine singular form *bel* and *nouvel* when they come before a noun beginning with a vowel or an *h*, for example

un bel appartement	*a beautiful flat*
un nouvel homme	*a new man*

Some adjectives never agree and these tend to be colours which are based on an original noun such as *marron* – *brown/chestnut* or *orange* – *orange* or those based on foreign words. Colours which are altered or qualified such as *brun foncé* – *dark brown* or *bleu clair* – *light blue* are invariable.

1.3 Comparison

In English we use two different strategies for the process of comparison of adjectives. These reflect the Germanic and Romance influences on English. One strategy involves the addition of the suffixes *–er* and *–est* to the basic form of the adjective as for example in *big* – *bigger* – *biggest* and is very similar to modern German. The other strategy is used with words with a greater number of syllables, for example *interesting* – *more* *interesting* – *most interesting* and is almost the exact equivalent of what happens in modern French:

big	*bigger*	*biggest*
grand	*plus grand*	*le plus grand*
interesting	*more interesting*	*most interesting*
intéressant	*plus intéressant*	*le, la, les plus intéressant(e)(s)*

All adjectives in French with the exception of two form their comparative and superlative in this way. The exceptions are *bon (good)* and *mauvais (bad)*. These two go as follows:

bon	*meilleur*	*le, la, les meilleur(e)(s)*
mauvais	*pire*	*le, la, les pire(s)*

Mauvais can also follow the regular pattern and be:

mauvais	*plus mauvais*	*le, la, les plus mauvais(e)(s)*

1.4 Adjectives with an infinitive or clause

There is a group of adjectives which often deal with a quality or an opinion such as *facile (easy)*, *intéressant (interesting)*, *agréable (pleasant)* which are involved in different constructions in a predictable and regular way. For example, let us take *difficile (difficult)*. The following are four related constructions in English:

Learning French is difficult
It is difficult to learn French
(Yes,) it/that is difficult
It/that is difficult to do

In the first example it is the process of *learning French* which is the subject of the verb *is*. In the second one there is the impersonal or dummy subject *it* which is subject of the verb *is*. In the third one, the *it* which is subject of *is* refers to something, probably *learning French* and so is not an impersonal dummy subject and can be replaced by *that*.

In the final one again, the *it* subject is not impersonal and can also be replaced by *that* as well as being followed by an infinitive which **cannot** have an object.

These three related structures are treated in a different but predictable way in French. Here they are again with their translations:

Learning French is difficult	*Apprendre le français est difficile*
It is difficult to learn French	*Il (c') est difficile **d**'apprendre le français*
(Yes,) it/that is difficult	*(Oui,) c'est difficile*
It/that is difficult to do	*C'est difficile **à** faire*

The first pair is straightforward and presents no problems other than to note that where in English we use an *–ing* form of the verb, in French we must use an infinitive.

In the others, the problem for speakers of English learning French is the correct choice between *ce* and *il*, the equivalent of the English *it*, and the correct choice between the preposition *de* or *à* when introducing the following clause or infinitive.

Concerning the choice between *ce* and *il* we need to know whether or not the *it* in English is actually referring to anything. An easy way to check this as shown in the examples above is to see whether the *it* can be replaced by *that* and still be grammatical and mean the same thing. In the last two examples this is clearly the case as there is no problem with the meaning of either alternative:

(Yes,) it/that is difficult	*(Oui,) c'est difficile*
It/that is difficult to do	*C'est difficile **à** faire*

Here the *it/that* is actually referring to something which is *difficult*.

However, with the second example above, repeated here, it is not possible to have this alternation:

It is difficult to learn French	*Il (c') est difficile **d**'apprendre le français*
*That is difficult to learn French	

(The * symbol is a standard way to show that a sentence is ungrammatical.)

In this example the thing that is difficult is *to learn French* and the *it* is just a sort of dummy subject which is there because English sentences must have subjects – it does not refer to anything.

In French *ce* is used when it refers to something and the *it/that* option is available in English and strictly speaking *il* is used when it does not refer to anything and we cannot have the *it/that* option.

This is the official position and you should stick to this rule in writing if you can. However, it is very common in modern spoken French and increasingly in some written French too for either *il* or *ce* to be used here as shown by the brackets in the example. In fact in spoken French *ce* is predominant in this construction with many speakers.

So that deals with choice of pronoun. Having made the correct choice you need to choose between *à* and *de* to introduce the infinitive and this is easy if following the official position above because the formula will always be:

> *il*est ADJECTIVE *de* CLAUSE
> *c'*est ADJECTIVE *à* INFINITIVE

However, it is possible to have *il/elle* as subject in this latter sort of structure. If that is that case then the pronoun always refers to someone, a human, for example:

> *Il/elle est difficile à comprendre*   *He/she is difficult to understand*

Here are some more examples:

> *It is interesting to compare them*   *Il est intéressant de les comparer*
> *It's easy to understand*   *C'est facile à comprendre*
> *It is preferable to read it first*   *Il est préférable de le lire d'abord*

2.0 Adverbs

In this section I shall deal very briefly with the formation of adverbs. I refer the reader to the excellent treatment of the formation and use of Adverbs in Chapter 5 of Hawkins and Towell (2015).

Adverbs are words or expressions which give extra information about the process described by the verb or what is being said in a sentence in general. Typically they deal with the '**how, when, where and why**' of what is going on. So a sentence *She sang* can be augmented with a word or phrase saying 'how' *she sang* or 'when' *she sang*. For example *she sang* **badly in the morning.** Here we are just going to consider the method in French of producing adverbs from adjectives and some main exceptions to this method.

In English there is a productive process for forming adverbs from adjectives by adding the suffix *–ly* to an adjective as has been done in the example above, adding *–ly* to *bad* to produce *badly*.

In French there is similar process. Simply add the suffix *–ment* to the feminine form of the adjective. For example:

*heureux (happy/fortunate) – heureuse – heureuse**ment** (happily/fortunately)*

There are some variations of this basic method of adverb formation. For example adjectives ending in *–ant* and *–ent* remove this element and add *–amment* and *–emment* respectively:

constant	*constamment*	*constantly*
prudent	*prudemment*	*prudently/cautiously*

But *lent – slow* becomes *lentement – slowly*

Also there are some adverbs formed from adjectives which end in *–e* which use the suffix *–ément:*

énorme	*énormément*	*enormously*
intense	*intensément*	*intensely*

but

probable	*probablement*	*probably*

In French, however, this process of adverb formation from adjectives is used far less frequently than in English and an adverbial phrase involving *d'une manière (in a way)/ de façon(fashion/manner)* + adjective or *avec (with)* + the noun related to the adjective is used instead of a single adverb. For example:

frighteningly could be *d'une manière effrayante*

astonishingly could be *de façon étonnante*

charmingly could be *avec charme*

3.0 Articles and Partitives

English speakers learning French have difficulty knowing when to use definite articles, *le la les*, indefinite articles *un, une (des)*, the partitive articles *du, de l', de la, des* and the possessive article, *mon, ma, mes* etc (sometimes also known as the possessive adjective). English uses the equivalents rather differently. In this section I shall try to give some general guidelines to help with their use.

3.1 Definite Articles

French makes much greater use of the definite article *le, la, les* than English does and the contexts where the two languages differ just need to be learned.

Firstly when we use a noun to introduce or refer to a general concept such as *fishing, green tea, work* or *cars* and then go on to say something about them, either as subject or object, in English we need no article:

Fishing is boring	*La pêche est ennuyeuse*
Green tea is good for health	*Le thé vert est bon pour la santé*
Work is important	*Le travail est important*
I don't like cars	*Je n'aime pas les voitures*

In each of these pairings there is no article in English but there must be one in French. The same holds true for abstract nouns, languages and countries:

love	*l'amour*
fear	*la peur*
hope	*l'espoir*
German	*l'allemand*
French	*le français*
Italian	*l'italian*
Brazil	*le Brézil*
Japan	*le Japon*
France	*la France*

Another context where French uses a definite article and English does not is the case of so-called 'inalienable possession'. This refers to parts of the body usually in examples such as:

I broke my arm	*Je me suis cassé **le** bras*
He twisted his ankle	*Il s'est tordu **la** cheville*
I brushed my teeth	*Je me suis brossé **les** dents*

In these examples, English uses a possessive adjective to show whose *arm* or *ankle* was damaged. French uses the indirect object reflexive pronoun to show whose *arm* or *ankle* was damaged and so there is no need of a possessive pronoun in French and a definite article is used instead. The first example cashes out to mean something like "*I broke to myself the arm*".

Other examples not involving the reflexive construction are:

He raised his hand	*Il a levé la main*
She lowered her eyes	*Elle a baissé les yeux*

Another use of the definite article which does not exist in English is where we wish to express habitual timings for events when we use the preposition *on* or *in* with a day or part of a day:

on Saturdays	*le samedi*
at the weekend	*le weekend*
in the evening	*le soir*
in the afternoon	*l'après-midi*

The French equivalent never has a preposition.

3.2 Partitive Articles and the Indefinite Article

In this section we need to consider how we put *some, a* and *an* into French.

3.2.1 Partitive articles

When dealing with an unspecified quantity of a substance or a quality such as *courage* the French use the partitive article *du, de l', de la* or *des*. Often this equates to the English word *some* or *any* in questions but not always because we leave it out frequently as in *I have got (some) problems*. Let us consider a few examples:

Would you like (some/any) bread?	*Voudrais-tu du pain?*
He has courage	*Il a du courage*
She has got (some) problems	*Elle a des problèmes*
Do you want (some/any) wine?	*Veux-tu du vin?*
I would like (some) help	*Je voudrais de l'aide*

However as soon as we start to be more specific with quantities, we move away from the partitive article and use the quantifier such as a number or perhaps *beaucoup* or *pas mal* both of which mean *a lot* followed by plain *de*. For example:

Would you like a slice of bread?	*Voudrais-tu une tranche de pain?*
He has a lot of courage	*Il a beaucoup de courage*
She has got lots of problems	*Elle a pas mal de problèmes*
Do you want a glass of wine?	*Veux-tu un verre de vin?*
I would like a little help	*Je voudrais un peu d'aide*

Nevertheless if you go on to say something more about the object or quality which is already defined or known about, you can sometimes use the partitive article after specific quantities:

*I bought a bottle **of the wine that you recommended***
*J'ai acheté une bouteille **du vin que tu as recommandé***

***A lot of the** problems are his fault (*you know about a specific set*)*
***Beaucoup des** problèmes sont de sa faute*

Contrast this with:

> **A lot of** *problems are his fault (*problems in general*)*
> **Beaucoup de** *problèmes sont de sa faute*

3.2.2 The Indefinite Article

There is a good deal of overlap in the usage of the indefinite article *un, une* in French and *a, an* in English and so in this section I shall mention two obvious areas in which there is difference.

The first difference is in negation. Consider the following pair of English sentences:

> *I have a pen*
> *I do not have a pen*

Here the indefinite article appears in both sentences. In French this is not the case:

> *J'ai un stylo*
> *Je n'ai pas **de** stylo*

In negative sentences in French, the indefinite article does not appear after *pas, jamais, plus* etc or any of the negative completers. It is just possible to allow the definite article to appear after *pas,* etc but this is very unusual and has the effect of really emphasizing the negation as in:

> *Je n'ai pas **un** Euro*   *I haven't a (single) Euro*

This is very limited and so in normal, neutral language avoid it and stick with *pas de.*

The second difference is after verbs such as *être, devenir, rester* when talking about professions or status. In English when asked what I do, I reply *I am **a** teacher.* In French in such a context the indefinite article must not appear and so the equivalent is *je suis professeur.* Here are some more examples:

> *He became an engineer*   *Il est devenu ingénieur*
> *She was a writer*   *Elle était écrivain*
> *He remained headmaster*   *Il est resté directeur de l'école*

The only exception to this is where the noun is modified by an adjective, or when the sentence begins with *c'est*, for example:

> *He was an exceptional teacher*   *Il était un professeur exceptional*
> *He is a doctor*   *C'est un médecin/Il est médecin*

3.3 Possessive Articles

Possessive articles in English are words such as *my, your,* etc given in the table below which cannot stand alone but have to come in front of a noun and they contrast with the possessive pronouns *mine, yours,* etc which can stand alone and are full pronouns (see Chapter 3 section 7.0).

Putting possessive articles into French poses two problems for speakers of English. Firstly, as you see in the table below, you have to choose between three French counterparts. Secondly, there are no separate words for *his/her/its*.

Possessive Articles (sometimes also called possessive adjectives)						
	my	*your*	*his/her/its*	*our*	*your*	*their*
Masculine	mon	ton	son	notre	votre	leur
Feminine	ma	ta	sa	notre	votre	leur
Plural	mes	tes	ses	nos	vos	leurs

Let us look at these two issues.

Firstly, the correct choice for French equivalent of *my* for example depends on the gender and number of the noun which follows it. So we have:

> *my father*   *mon père*
> *my mother*   *ma mère*
> *my parents*   *mes parents*

The choice of word does not depend on the sex of the speaker. A son would say *ma mère* and a daughter would say *mon père*. The same goes for all of these possessive articles. Make the word agree with the noun which follows in both gender and number.

Secondly, with the problem of *his/her/its* each of the French alternatives can mean *his/her/its*. For example, in isolation we cannot tell what *son père* means because we do not know the context. In English we will only use words such as *his/her/its* when we know who we are talking about and the same is true in French when using *son/sa/ses*.

We choose *son* to go with *père* because *père* is masculine singular in the same way that we choose *mon* to go with *père* in the above examples. *Mon* does not reflect the gender of the 'possessor' and in the same way *son* does not either. So we just have to accept that *son, sa* and *ses* can **each** mean *his/her/its*.

If you need to stress that you are talking about **his** *father* as opposed to **her** *father* you can say *son père à lui* as opposed to *son père à elle,* making use of the masculine and feminine emphatic pronouns (See Chapter 3, section 2.3) to stress the difference.

Here are some examples:

my house	*ma maison (feminine singular)*
his book	*son livre (masculine singular)*
her book	*son livre (masculine singular)*
their friends	*leurs amis (plural)*
your aunt	*ta tante (feminine singular)*
his problems	*ses problèmes (plural)*
her examples	*ses exemples (plural)*

As you see all of these possessive articles agree with the following noun and not with the person possessing the thing.

Chapter 5

The Primacy of Spoken French

Eugène Ionesco began to write plays as a result of trying to learn English from a book. Soon he realised that he was not learning a system of communication but a series of dry sentences and astoundingly obvious truths such as 'the ceiling is above us and the floor is below us' where there is no communication at all. The method that he was using involved the repetition of sentences.

It was the evident lack of communication which prompted him to write *La Cantatrice Chauve*, his first and most explosive play in which the characters talk at and contradict each other and themselves. The end result is a complete breakdown of language and a cacophony of sound. In his second play *La Leçon* an initially gentle teacher transforms into an oppressive killer subduing a vivacious young pupil with words, ending up repeating the word *'cou-teau'* *'kn-ife'*. The maid in the play warns us all that *'la philologie mène au pire'* ('*philology [study of language] leads to the worst*'), a warning which we must all take seriously!

In this book so far we have been looking at the core processes of the grammar of formal, written French so that English speaking learners can have a base knowledge of the norms of French grammar from which to launch themselves into the language proper. As a result we have been building up a knowledge of a very correct official version of the language which has its place in certain contexts and registers.

In any language there are different levels and styles depending on the context of use, whether it is written or spoken, formal or informal or among friends. In French this is just as much true as in any language and in what follows I am going to consider some of the more obvious elements of variation from the standards and norms of grammatical behaviour considered so far. The collection of test sentences which accompany the different sections of this book runs the danger of falling into the same category as the sentences which inspired Ionesco and I am keen to offset that by pointing out that real spoken language is often very different. In what follows I wish to highlight some of the ways in which the spoken language can differ from the formal written norm in three of the areas which I have covered so far.

1.0 Negation

The classic rules for negation in French given above in Chapter 2 section 4.0, involving the negative particle *ne* placed before the tensed verb and any pronoun objects which there might be followed by a negative completer such as *pas, plus, jamais,* etc are more often than not broken in the spoken language. Quite simply the *ne* just does not appear and so we have examples such as:

je sais pas	*I don't know*
(il) y a pas	*there isn't*
j'ai rien entendu	*I didn't hear anything*
(il) faut pas dire ça	*you mustn't say that*

These examples are the norm for the spoken everyday informal language where it would be unusual to hear their standard equivalents formed according to the classic rules of negation:

je ne sais pas	*I do not know*
il n' y a pas	*there is not*
je n'ai rien entendu	*I did not hear anything*
il ne faut pas dire ça	*you must not say that*

The English translations given here compared with the English translations given above give something of the flavour of the contrast between the two different sets.

The variation in use of these forms is dependent on context or register and level or social (educational) status of the speaker. According to Rouayrenc (2010) there are some speakers who will use only the more informal version but there are no speakers who use only the formal version. Those of higher social or educational status who are more likely to use the full formal version of negation use the informal version in less formal contexts or registers.

In general the omission of *ne* is dependent on a variety of factors; type of subject, type of verb, tense of verb and type of negation.

Informal negation is likely to be used much more if the subject is a pronoun, for example *c', ça, il,* but it tends mainly to be the third person pronouns; it is less common with *nous* and *vous* but does exist, for example:

nous avons pas fini	*we haven't finished*
vous avez pas fini de jacasser comme ça?	*will you stop chattering!*

It is also less common with full noun subjects.

As for types of verb and tenses, informal negation is most frequently found with *être, avoir, falloir* and the more common verbs and with the present and perfect tenses, although this is just a tendency and it can be found with a wide variety of verbs and tenses.

Informal negation is predominantly found with standard negation involving *pas* but is very common also with other negative completers such as *jamais* and *plus*:

Je sais plus	*I don't know any more*
Elle est jamais allée en Italie	*She's never been to Italy*

See Rouayrenc (2010) for much more detailed discussion and illustration of this where the work is based on extensive corpora of real recorded French.

2.0 Questions

The standard methods of question formation given in Chapter 2 section 3.0 are inversion of subject and verb and the use of *est-ce que*. I did not mention then a very common and in fact standard method used exclusively in speech and that is simply to use rising intonation on an ordinary statement:

Tu aimes le poulet	*You like chicken*
Tu aimes le poulet?	*Do you like chicken?*

In writing this can only be expressed by the addition of a question mark after the statement. This method is acknowledged as standard and is given in most text books.

It emerges from the study of corpora that the intonation method is probably the most common in speech followed by the use of *est-ce que*, with inversion being in third place. The rarest form is inversion used when there is a full noun and a related pronoun of the following sort:

Mon frère, est-il arrivé?	*My brother, has he arrived?*

For **Yes/No** questions these are the main methods of question formation. For the equivalent *wh-* questions in French, there is much greater variety. The following is taken from Detey, Durand, Laks and Lyche (2010):

Où est-ce qu'il va? Il va où? Où il va? Où va-t-il? Où est-ce que c'est qu'il va? Où c'est qu'il va? C'est où qu'il va? Où c'est que c'est qu'il va? Où qu'il va? Où que c'est qu'il va?

This wide variety of forms some standard, some non-standard are very commonly used, all meaning *Where is he going?*

One line sticks in my mind from the film *Ne le dis à Personne* (*Tell No One*) where the character Bruno twice yells at one of the villains:

Pour qui tu bosses?   *Who are you working for?*

3.0 Passive

N. Rossi-Gensane notes in Detey, Durand, Laks and Lyche (2010) that what she calls *"les passifs scolaires"* such as *la souris est mangée par le chat – the mouse is eaten by the cat* are rare in spontaneous speech. This is essentially the sort of passive described in Chapter 2 section 1.0 where it is noted that this construction is used much less often in French than in English in general. In speech this is all the more so than in writing.

One alternative frequently used is to keep the sentence active and simply suppress the original agent, making it vague by replacing it by *on*. Compare this to the official passive construction where the agent can be present or not in the *par*-phrase:

> *Jean a cassé la fenêtre*   *John broke the window*
> *On a cassé la fenêtre*   *Someone broke the window*
> *La fenêtre a été cassée (par Jean)*   *The window has been broken (by John)*

Another is to use a reflexive construction where expression of the agent is completely suppressed, no *par*-phrase being possible:

> *La fenêtre s'est cassée*   *The window broke*

A third possibility when the original active object is human is to use a reflexive version of *laisser, faire, voir, entendre* plus an infinitive (examples from Rouayrenc (2010)):

> *Il s'est laissé entraîner par ses copains*
> *Il s'est fait aider par ses copains*

These are equivalent to *he let himself be dragged along by his friends* and *he got himself helped by his friends*, the latter showing some element of volition on **his** part.

> *Il s'est entendu reprocher son égoïsme par ses enfants*
> *Il s'est vu critiquer par ses adversaires*

These are literally equivalent to *he heard himself reproached for his egoism by his children* and *he saw himself criticised by his opponents*. In both the subject is represented as being a bystander to some extent. Both would be translated into English by a standard passive: *he was reproached, he was criticised...*

These alternatives to the passive appear in speech much more frequently than the *passif scolaire*.

There are of course very many other areas where the spoken language differs sometimes considerably from the official written norm. It is not the purpose of the current work to cover them all. What I have wished to do here is to point out that what I have provided in most of this book is a starting point from which to explore the language much more fully. There is a rich literature on the subject and I would encourage the reader to look at Rouayrenc (2010) and Detey, Durand, Laks and Lyche (2010) to increase their awareness of this important issue.

Appendix 1: Irregular Present Tense Verbs

The following are the 48 most common irregular verbs in the Present Tense

Aller	-	*to go*
S'asseoir	-	*to sit down*
Avoir	-	*to have*
Battre	-	*to beat/hit*
Boire	-	*to drink*
Conclure	-	*to conclude*
Connaître	-	*to know*
Coudre	-	*to sew*
Courir	-	*to run*
Craindre	-	*to fear*
Croire	-	*to believe*
Croître	-	*to grow*
Cueillir	-	*to pick*
Cuire	-	*to cook*
Devoir	-	*to have to/must OR to owe*
Dire	-	*to say*
Dormir	-	*to sleep*
Écrire	-	*to write*
Envoyer	-	*to send*
Être	-	*to be*
Faire	-	*to do/make*
Falloir	-	*to be necessary (il form only)*
Fuir	-	*to flee/run away*
Haïr	-	*to hate*
Joindre	-	*to join*
Lire	-	*to read*
Mettre	-	*to put/put on*
Mourir	-	*to die*
Mouvoir	-	*to move*
Naître	-	*to be born*
Ouvrir	-	*to open*
Peindre	-	*to paint*
Plaire	-	*to please*
Pleuvoir	-	*to rain (il form only)*
Pouvoir	-	*can/ to be able*
Prendre	-	*to take*
Recevoir	-	*to receive*
Rire	-	*to laugh*
Savoir	-	*to know*
Sentir	-	*to feel/ to smell of something*
Servir	-	*to serve/ to be used as*
Suivre	-	*to follow*
Tenir	-	*to hold*
Vaincre	-	*to conquer*
Venir	-	*to come*
Vivre	-	*to live*
Voir	-	*to see*
Vouloir	-	*to wish/want*

I. The First 8.

Aller	-	to go	
		Je vais	Nous allons
		Tu vas	Vous allez
		Il/Elle va	Ils/Elles vont

S'asseoir	-	to sit down	
		Je m'assieds	Nous nous asseyons
		Tu t'assieds	Vous vous asseyez
		Il/Elle s'assied	Ils/Elles s'asseyent

Avoir	-	to have	
		J'ai	Nous avons
		Tu as	Vous avez
		Il/Elle a	Ils/Elles ont

Battre	-	to beat/hit	
		Je bats	Nous battons
		Tu bats	Vous battez
		Il/Elle bat	Ils/Elles battent

Boire	-	to drink	
		Je bois	Nous buvons
		Tu bois	Vous buvez
		Il/Elle boit	Ils/Elles boivent

Conclure	-	to conclude	
		Je conclus	Nous concluons
		Tu conclus	Vous concluez
		Il/Elle conclut	Ils/Elles concluent

Connaître	-	to know	
		Je connais	Nous connaissons
		Tu connais	Vous connaissez
		Il/Elle connaît	Ils/Elles connaissent

Coudre	-	to sew	
		Je couds	Nous cousons
		Tu couds	Vous cousez
		Il/Elle coud	Ils/Elles cousent

II. The Second 8.

Courir   -   *to run*

     Je cours   *Nous courons*
     Tu cours   *Vous courez*
     Il/Elle court   *Ils/Elles courent*

Craindre   -   *to fear*

     Je crains   *Nous craignons*
     Tu crains   *Vous craignez*
     Il/Elle craint   *Ils/Elles craignent*

Croire   -   *to believe*

     Je crois   *Nous croyons*
     Tu crois   *Vous croyez*
     Il/Elle croit   *Ils/Elles croient*

Croître   -   *to grow*

     Je croîs   *Nous croissons*
     Tu croîs   *Vous croissez*
     Il/Elle croît   *Ils/Elles croissent*

Cueillir   -   *to pick*

     Je cueille   *Nous cueillons*
     Tu cueilles   *Vous cueillez*
     Il/Elle cueille   *Ils/Elles cueillent*

Cuire   -   *to cook*

     Je cuis   *Nous cuisons*
     Tu cuis   *Vous cuisez*
     Il/Elle cuit   *Ils/Elles cuisent*

Devoir   -   *to have to/must OR to owe*

     Je dois   *Nous devons*
     Tu dois   *Vous devez*
     Il/Elle doit   *Ils/elles doivent*

Dire   -   *to say*

     Je dis   *Nous disons*
     Tu dis   *Vous dîtes*
     Il/Elle dit   *Ils/Elles disent*

III. The Third 8.

Dormir   -   to sleep
                         Je dors   Nous dormons
                         Tu dors   Vous dormez
                         Il/Elle dort   Ils/Elles dorment

Écrire   -   to write
                         J'écris   Nous écrivons
                         Tu écris   Vous écrivez
                         Il/Elle écrit   Ils/Elles écrivent

Envoyer   -   to send
                         J'envoie   Nous envoyons
                         Tu envoies   Vous envoyez
                         Il/Elle envoie   Ils/Elles envoient

Être   -   to be
                         Je suis   Nous sommes
                         Tu es   Vous êtes
                         Il/Elle est   Ils/Elles sont

Faire   -   to do/make
                         Je fais   Nous faisons
                         Tu fais   Vous faites
                         Il/Elle fait   Ils/Elles font

Falloir   -   to be necessary (il form only)
                         Il faut

Fuir   -   to flee/run away/leak
                         Je fuis   Nous fuyons
                         Tu fuis   Vous fuyez
                         Il/Elle fuit   Ils/Elles fuient

Haïr   -   to hate
                         Je hais   Nous haïssons
                         Tu hais   Vous haïssez
                         Il/Elle hait   Ils/Elles haïssent

IV. The Fourth 8.

Joindre   -   to join
         Je joins   Nous joignons
         Tu joins   Vous joignez
         Il/Elle joint   Ils/Elles joignent

Lire   -   to read
         Je lis   Nous lisons
         Tu lis   Vous lisez
         Il/Elle lit   Ils/Elles lisent

Mettre   -   to put/put on
         Je mets   Nous mettons
         Tu mets   Vous mettez
         Il/Elle met   Ils/Elles mettent

Mourir   -   to die
         Je meurs   Nous mourons
         Tu meurs   Vous mourez
         Il/Elle meurt   Ils/Elles meurent

Mouvoir   -   to move
         Je meus   Nous mouvons
         Tu meus   Vous mouvez
         Il/Elle meut   Ils/Elles meuvent

Naître   -   to be born
         Je nais   Nous naissons
         Tu nais   Vous naissez
         Il/Elle naît   Ils/Elles/naissent

Ouvrir   -   to open
         J'ouvre   Nous ouvrons
         Tu ouvres   Vous ouvrez
         Il/Elle ouvre   Ils/Elles ouvrent

Peindre   -   to paint
         Je peins   Nous peignons
         Tu peins   Vous peignez
         Il/Elle peint   Ils/Elles peignent

V. The Fifth 8.

Plaire	-	*to please*	
		Je plais	*Nous plaisons*
		Tu plais	*Vous plaisez*
		Il/Elle plaît	*Ils/Elles plaisent*

Pleuvoir	-	*to rain (il form only)*	
		Il pleut	

Pouvoir	-	*can/ to be able*	
		Je peux	*Nous pouvons*
		Tu peux	*Vous pouvez*
		Il/Elle peut	*Ils/Elles peuvent*

Prendre	-	*to take*	
		Je prends	*Nous prenons*
		Tu prends	*Vous prenez*
		Il/Elle prend	*Ils/Elles prennent*

Recevoir	-	*to receive*	
		Je reçois	*Nous recevons*
		Tu reçois	*Vous recevez*
		Il/Elle reçoit	*Ils/Elles reçoivent*

Rire	-	*to laugh*	
		Je ris	*Nous rions*
		Tu ris	*Vous riez*
		Il/Elle rit	*Ils/Elles rient*

Savoir	-	*to know*	
		Je sais	*Nous savons*
		Tu sais	*Vous savez*
		Il/Elle sait	*Ils/Elles savent*

Sentir	-	*to feel/ to smell of something*	
		Je sens	*Nous sentons*
		Tu sens	*Vous sentez*
		Il/Elle sent	*Ils/Elles sentent*

VI. The Sixth 8.

Servir	-	*to serve/ to be used as*	
		Je sers	*Nous servons*
		Tu sers	*Vous servez*
		Il/Elle sert	*Ils/Elles servent*
Suivre	-	*to follow*	
		Je suis	*Nous suivons*
		Tu suis	*Vous suivez*
		Il/Elle suit	*Ils/Elles suivent*
Tenir	-	*to hold*	
		Je tiens	*Nous tenons*
		Tu tiens	*Vous tenez*
		Il/Elle tient	*Ils/Elles tiennent*
Vaincre	-	*to conquer*	
		Je vaincs	*Nous vainquons*
		Tu vaincs	*Vous vainquez*
		Il/Elle vainc	*Ils/Elles vainquent*
Venir	-	*to come*	
		Je viens	*Nous venons*
		Tu viens	*Vous venez*
		Il/Elle vient	*Ils/Elles viennent*
Vivre	-	*to live*	
		Je vis	*Nous vivons*
		Tu vis	*Vous vivez*
		Il/Elle vit	*Ils/Elles vivent*
Voir	-	*to see*	
		Je vois	*Nous voyons*
		Tu vois	*Vous voyez*
		Il/Elle voit	*Ils/Elles voient*
Vouloir	-	*to wish/want*	
		Je veux	*Nous voulons*
		Tu veux	*Vous voulez*
		Il/Elle veut	*Ils/Elles veulent*

Appendix 2: Irregular Past Participles

Infinitive	Past Participle	Meaning
asseoir	assis	to sit
avoir	eu	to have
boire	bu	to drink
conclure	conclu	to conclude
conduire	conduit	to drive
connaître	connu	to know
construire	construit	to build
coudre	cousu	to sew
courir	couru	to run
couvrir	couvert	to cover
craindre	craint	to fear
croire	cru	to believe
croître	crû	to grow
cuire	cuit	to cook
devoir	dû	to have to
dire	dit	to say
écrire	écrit	to write
être	été	to be
faire	fait	to do/make
falloir	fallu	to be necessary
haïr	haï	to hate
joindre	joint	to join
lire	lu	to read
mettre	mis	to put
mourir	mort	to die
mouvoir	mû	to move
naître	né	to be born
offrir	offert	to offer
ouvrir	ouvert	to open
paraître	paru	to appear/seem
peindre	peint	to paint
plaire	plu	to please
pleuvoir	plu	to rain
pouvoir	pu	to be able
prendre	pris	to take
recevoir	reçu	to receive
rire	ri	to laugh
savoir	su	to know
souffrir	souffert	to suffer
suivre	suivi	to follow
se taire	se tu	to be silent
tenir	tenu	to hold
vaincre	vaincu	to vanquish
valoir	valu	to be worth
venir	venu	to come
vivre	vécu	to live
voir	vu	to see
vouloir	voulu	to wish/want

Appendix 3: Verbs and Infinitives

In the lists below, I have put the dummy verb *faire* to represent any verb which follows and in the list of verbs with indirect objects, *qn* stands for *quelq'un – someone*.

You just have to learn these patterns. They are not the only ones but they are a good starting point.

With *à*:

aider à faire	to help to do
arriver à faire	to manage to do
s'attendre à faire	to expect to do
chercher à faire	to attempt to do
commencer à faire	to begin to do
continuer à faire	to continue doing/to do
se décider à faire	to make up one's mind to do
encourager à faire	to encourage to do
hésiter à faire	to hesitate to do
inviter à faire	to invite to do
renoncer à faire	to give up doing
réussir à faire	to succeed in doing

With *de*:

accuser de faire	to accuse of doing
s'arrêter de faire	to stop doing
avoir besoin de faire	to need to do
avoir peur de faire	to be afraid of doing
cesser de faire	to stop (cease) doing
décider de faire	to decide to do
empêcher de faire	to prevent from doing
essayer de faire	to try to do
éviter de faire	to avoid doing
finir de faire	to finish doing
menacer de faire	to threaten to do
offrir de faire	to offer to do
oublier de faire	to forget to do
refuser de faire	to refuse to do
tenter de faire	to attempt to do

With Indirect Objects:

conseiller à qn de faire	*to advise someone to do*
défendre à qn de faire	*to forbid someone to do*
demander à qn de faire	*to ask someone to do*
dire à qn de faire	*to tell someone to do*
permettre à qn de faire	*to permit someone to do*
promettre à qn de faire	*to promise to do*

With [0] (nothing):

aimer faire	*to like to do (doing)*
aimer mieux faire	*to prefer to do (doing)*
aller faire	*to go and do*
désirer faire	*to desire to do*
devoir faire	*to have to do*
espérer faire	*to hope to do*
laisser faire	*to let (allow to) do*
oser faire	*to dare to do*
pouvoir faire	*to be able to do*
préférer faire	*to prefer to do*
savoir faire	*to know how to do*
sembler faire	*to seem to do*
vouloir faire	*to wish/want to do*

Sentences for Translation

Irregular Present Tense

Translate into French

1. They are writing
2. She reads
3. We do not believe
4. They want
5. He serves
6. I am laughing
7. Do you (Vous) see?
8. You (Tu) do not take
9. We are sewing
10. I conclude
11. My uncle runs
12. She beats the dog
13. We believe the story
14. You (Tu) are sleeping well
15. They are reading the paper

Future and Conditional Tense sentences

Translate into French

Future Tense

1. *She will finish at 6*
2. *The president will have to leave*
3. *I will send the letter*
4. *You (Vous) will run*
5. *He will see his brother*
6. *We will be happy*
7. *They will have lunch at 14.00*
8. *You (Vous) will know the answer*
9. *They will not come to school*
10. *It will rain*

Conditional Tense

1. *I would finish my lunch*
2. *She would go to London*
3. *We would like to leave*
4. *He would do nothing*
5. *They would leave*
6. *You (Vous) would know (Savoir)*
7. *They would be happy*
8. *I would send the letter*
9. *My sister would have to leave*
10. *They would come to the house*

Perfect Tense sentences

Translate into French

1. *We read the book*
2. *She went to the library*
3. *They have eaten the cheese*
4. *Have you seen the books?*
5. *They (Masc) arrived at 8.00*
6. *The girls stayed in the house*
7. *My brother has read the letter*
8. *She left at 7.00*
9. *His father built a house*
10. *I did nothing*

Further Compound Tense sentences

Translate into French

1. *They had left*
2. *My friends will have opened the present*
3. *She would have understood*
4. *I had written the letter*
5. *I would have believed you (Te)*
6. *They would have been able to leave*
7. *You (Tu) had said nothing*
8. *We would have read the paper*
9. *They (Fem) will have returned*
10. *Her sisters had fallen*

Compound Tense Past Participle Agreement sentences

Translate into French

I. Être verb agreement
1. She arrived at 6.00
2. The girls stayed in the house
3. We (Masc) left after the play
4. She would have gone to the match
5. They (Fem) had fallen

II. PDO – Object Pronouns
1. We saw them (Masc)
2. I met her at the station
3. He would have liked them (Fem)
4. Your (Tes) books? Yes I have sold them
5. She had understood them (Fem)

III. PDO – Object Antecedent in Relative construction.
1. She is a woman that I met last year
2. These are books which I had read
3. These are problems which I would have understood
4. Here is the window which he broke
5. I like the stories which he wrote

IV. PDO – Wh- object questions – (use Tu)
1. Which window did you break?
2. Which books did you buy?
3. Which wine did you prefer?
4. Which girls did you meet?
5. Which problems did you solve?

V. Reflexive agreement
1. The boys had got up at 6.00
2. They saw themselves in the mirror
3. She sent herself a letter
4. He would have got dressed
5. The girl surprised herself

Tense Chart sentences

Translate into French

1. *I am singing*
2. *She eats*
3. *You (Tu) are selling*
4. *We have gone*
5. *They (Masc) have been talking*
6. *He has been learning French for three years*
7. *I bought a boat yesterday*
8. *We went to Brighton each Saturday*
9. *It was sunny*
10. *We were eating lunch*
11. *I used to play the banjo*
12. *She had finished the book*
13. *They had been sleeping*
14. *He had been talking for five minutes*
15. *We will go to the theatre tomorrow*
16. *You (Vous) will be arriving in ten minutes*
17. *They will understand*
18. *He would finish at seven o'clock*
19. *I would be very happy*
20. *I would be swimming, if....*
21. *We have known them for years*
22. *When I am older I shall buy a motorbike*
23. *They will come home when they have finished their work*
24. *When we arrived he had been there for two hours*
25. *I have been talking for ten minutes*

Past Historic and Past Anterior sentences

Translate into English

1. *Il fut surpris de les voir*
2. *Le duc entra dans le château*
3. *Quand ils eurent mangé leur repas, les élèves finirent leurs devoirs*
4. *Ils les virent au bout de la rue*
5. *Elle perdit son mouchoir*
6. *Aussitôt qu'ils furent arrivés dans le bourg, ils vinrent à l'église*
7. *Soudain elles eurent froid*
8. *Il entendit siffler le train*
9. *Soudain je vis un ours énorme*
10. *« Absolument pas ! » répondit-il*

Passive sentences

Translate into French

1. *He was noticed by everyone*
2. *A letter will be sent tomorrow*
3. *The window was broken by the explosion*
4. *The table had been repaired by the carpenter*
5. *We will be welcomed by the mayor*
6. *They were given a book*
7. *The door was opened (The door opened)*
8. *We will be sent the information*
9. *That just is not done*
10. *He was told the right answer*

Imperative sentences

1. *Write the letter. (Vous)*
2. *Sing that song. (Tu)*
3. *Let's finish the film.*
4. *Do not talk. (Tu)*
5. *Hide them! (Tu)*
6. *Don't hide them! (Vous)*
7. *Give me the book. (Tu)*
8. *Don't give him the book. (Tu)*
9. *Get up! (Tu)*
10. *Don't get dressed! (Vous)*

Question sentences

Translate into French

1. *Does he speak French?*
2. *Will you be at the party? (Tu)*
3. *Does your mother like your friends?*
4. *When did you arrive? (Tu)*
5. *Which books did you like? (Tu)*
6. *Why will they (Masc) be at the meal?*
7. *Who did you sent the present to? (Tu)*
8. *Did they (Fem) like the play?*
9. *(At) what time will they (Masc) set off?*
10. *Was your brother watching that film?*

Negative sentences

Translate into French

1. *I don't know*
2. *He had not finished*
3. *We will not go on holiday this year*
4. *My parents did not understand the problem*
5. *I have not got a sister*
6. *I know nothing*
7. *I have never travelled to Italy*
8. *We only have 30 Euros*
9. *No one understands*
10. *Nothing is important*

Verbs and Infinitives sentences

Translate into French

1.   We tried to understand
2.   I prefer fishing
3.   My father decided to buy that house
4.   He seems to understand the problem
5.   I asked my teacher to explain the question
6.   He refused to try to stop smoking
7.   We have to go now
8.   She made up her mind to try to learn German
9.   I hope to go to Italy in the summer
10. He told us to arrive at 7.00

Reflexive verb sentences

Translate into French

1. *She injured herself*
2. *We will have fun*
3. *We bought presents for each other*
4. *They (Masc) know each other*
5. *This wine is drunk with beef*
6. *That is understood*
7. *He deals with guests*
8. *She made fun of the teacher*
9. *You will cut your finger (Tu)*
10. *He washed his face*

Subjunctive sentences

Translate into French

1. *It is necessary that we eat at 7.00*
2. *Even though it is a short journey,....*
3. *It seems that they understand*
4. *They are waiting for us to leave*
5. *I want you (Tu) to leave now*
6. *They bought it without us knowing*
7. *I am sorry that you (Tu) are selling the house*
8. *She is the best singer that I know*
9. *I am happy that you're (Tu) here*
10. *They want me to become president*
11. *He is happy that I have finished the book*
12. *It seems that they have understood*
13. *Even though she has met him,...*
14. *It is the best wine that I have tasted*
15. *I am sorry that you have not seen her*

Modal sentences

Translate into French

1. *They want to understand*
2. *She had wanted to leave at 7.00*
3. *They would have to read the book*
4. *You (Tu) will be able to finish on time*
5. *He must have left it in the car*
6. *We would have been able to watch the play*
7. *I ought to have washed the floor*
8. *She should have booked the room*
9. *We had to write an essay (Tense?)*
10. *He could have warned us of the danger*

Y Avoir sentences

Translate into French

1.   *There used to be a school here*
2.   *There will be problems*
3.   *Suddenly there was a loud noise*
4.   *There would have been a lot of people*
5.   *There must be a baker's near here*
6.   *There could be a problem*
7.   *There would be a good reason for that*
8.   *There are lots of apples*
9.   *There will have been a lot of noise*
10. *There must be a solution (Subjunctive?)*

Conditional Structure sentences

Translate into French

For these sentences where appropriate, the answers are given in the *Tu* form only

1. *If you do not go home now there will be problems*
2. *We would buy the house if we had enough money*
3. *If you write to your aunt she will give you some money*
4. *If you had listened you would have understood*
5. *You would have been able to leave on time if you had got up early*
6. *If you had arrived at 6 we would have eaten together*
7. *We will be pleased if you win*
8. *If you had left on time you would have arrived before the start of the match*
9. *If you want we will finish soon*
10. *If you learn all of this you will succeed*

Miscellaneous constructions

Present Participles and Après avoir/être + Past Participle

Translate into French:

1. *Surprising results*
2. *A tiring journey*
3. *An interesting girl*
4. *I discovered them eating chocolate*
5. *He opened the door talking noisily*
6. *I ate the cake while reading the paper*
7. *Having spoken to his sister he went home*
8. *When they had finished supper they watched the television*
9. *Having arrived she phoned her mother*
10. *When I had finished the work I went to the pub*

Il y a, venir de, être en train de, être sur le point de, depuis construction

Translate into French:

1. *I worked there seven years ago*
2. *She started her job two weeks ago*
3. *They (Masc) have just finished*
4. *We had just eaten when the priest arrived*
5. *I am in the middle of talking*
6. *He was in the middle of playing golf when it rained*
7. *We are about to leave*
8. *They (Fem) were about to go to sleep*
9. *I have been teaching here for twenty-five years*
10. *She had been sleeping for three hours*

Subject and object pronouns

1. She knows him
2. They like us
3. We told them a story
4. I sold it (fem) to her
5. Your parents? I have not seen them
6. Have you (Tu) met her?
7. Do it now! (Tu)
8. Watch me! (Tu)
9. Don't tell me it! (Tu)
10. I am happy with it (content de)
11. Come to the party? I did not invite them to it
12. We went there last year
13. Have some more cheese! No thanks I have already eaten enough
14. Here is a glass of wine. Yes I would like some/one
15. He left them (masc) there
16. She gave him it (masc) yesterday
17. We have already sent him some
18. He offered us them (fem)
19. I have thought about it (réfléchir à)
20. We will send them the keys

Emphatic, strong or stressable pronouns

1. *With them (masc)*
2. *For her*
3. *After him*
4. *Near me*
5. *Get up! (singular)*
6. *Show me your passport*
7. *Tell me the truth*
8. *Don't tell me the truth*
9. **__Him?__** *He is an idiot*
10. *It was they/them(fem) who arrived first*
11. *They did it themselves (masc)*
12. *He is more intelligent than you (singular)*
13. *She is better than him/he*
14. *My family and I are delighted*
15. *She and I bought it*

Relative pronouns

Basic relative structures in French

1. The man I met was old
2. The wine that I really like is from Bordeaux
3. The thing that surprised me was his hair
4. This is a problem which irritates me
5. What I prefer is fishing
6. What annoys me the most is greed
7. A squirrel is a rat which lives in the trees
8. I do not know what you mean
9. Tell me what has happened
10. She is someone who(m) I respect greatly

More complex relatives in French

1. The thing that I was happiest about was the lunch
2. It is something which I cannot understand the importance of
3. It is an animal which I am afraid of
4. He is a man who I have a great respect for
5. They are people for whom I would do anything
6. She is the woman I gave my book to
7. Music is something I cannot live without
8. This is the office where I work
9. A barrel is a container into which we pour beer
10. It is the moment after which they all leave

Interrogative, Demonstrative, Possessive and Indefinite pronouns

1. *What have you done? (Tu)*
2. *Who did that?*
3. *What did you buy yesterday? (Tu)*
4. *Have you read those books? Which one do you prefer? (Tu)*
5. *Which of those apples do you like? (Tu)*
6. *Of all of his plays, this one is my favourite*
7. *These trees are taller than those ones*
8. *This building is older than that one*
9. *When I use a pen I always choose this one*
10. *Did you use this coat or that one? (Tu)*
11. *Painting windows! Oh, I love that!*
12. *That's better now*
13. *This is important*
14. *That makes me laugh!*
15. *This is what I cannot understand*
16. *I like this house but I prefer mine*
17. *His photos are more interesting than hers*
18. *Our teacher is boring but have you heard theirs?*
19. *This cake is mine*
20. *It is hers not yours! (Tu)*

Adjective phrases and sentences

1. *The lawyer was dishonest*
2. *A dishonest lawyer*
3. *An old house*
4. *A happy child*
5. *A small child*
6. *The green dress*
7. *The former president*
8. *An ancient building*
9. *My own parents*
10. *A new flat*
11. *A happy life*
12. *A light blue shirt*
13. *A more exciting story*
14. *A better solution*
15. *The worst problem*
16. *It is difficult to understand chemistry*
17. *Yes, it is difficult to understand*
18. *It is important to work hard*
19. *Yes it is important*
20. *He is easy to understand*

Adverbs and Articles

1. *She spoke very clearly*
2. *They speak French fluently*
3. *My father drives slowly*
4. *He was enormously tall*
5. *They are probably there*
6. *He reacted intelligently*
7. *I love novels*
8. *Diesel is the most popular fuel*
9. *German is difficult*
10. *Cooperation is essential*
11. *My mother cut her finger*
12. *He cut his hair*
13. *I never work on Sunday*
14. *Have you got any change? (Tu)*
15. *Would you like some beer? (Tu)*
16. *He has patience*
17. *Would you like a glass of beer? (Tu)*
18. *She has a lot of talent*
19. *Can I have one of the books that you bought? (Tu)*
20. *I have not got a brother*
21. *They have no luck*
22. *His mother was a dancer*
23. *My son became a lion tamer*
24. *Her father is a lawyer*
25. *His father is a lawyer*

Answers

Irregular Present Tense answers

1. *Ils/elles écrivent*
2. *Elle lit*
3. *Nous ne croyons pas*
4. *Ils/elles veulent*
5. *Il sert*
6. *Je ris*
7. *Voyez-vous/Est-ce que vous voyez?*
8. *Tu ne prends pas*
9. *Nous cousons*
10. *Je conclus*
11. *Mon oncle court*
12. *Elle bat le chien*
13. *Nous croyons l'histoire*
14. *Tu dors bien*
15. *Ils/elles lisent le journal*

Future and Conditional Tense sentences answers

Future Tense sentences

1. *Elle finira à six heures*
2. *Le président devra partir*
3. *J'enverrai la lettre*
4. *Vous courrez*
5. *Il verra son frère*
6. *Nous serons contents*
7. *Ils/elles déjeuneront à 14.00*
8. *Vous saurez la réponse*
9. *Ils/elles ne viendront pas à l'école*
10. *Il pleuvra*

Conditional Tense sentences

1. *Je finirais mon déjeuner*
2. *Elle irait à Londres*
3. *Nous voudrions partir/nous aimerions partir*
4. *Il ne ferait rien*
5. *Ils/Elles partiraient*
6. *Vous sauriez*
7. *Ils/Elles seraient content(e)s*
8. *J'enverrais la lettre*
9. *Ma sœur devrait partir*
10. *Ils/Elles viendraient à la maison*

Perfect Tense sentences answers

1.   *Nous avons lu le livre*
2.   *Elle est allée à la bibliothèque*
3.   *Ils ont mangé le fromage*
4.   *As-tu/avez-vous vu les livres?*
5.   *Ils sont arrivés à huit heures*
6.   *Les filles sont restées dans la maison*
7.   *Mon frère a lu la lettre*
8.   *Elle est partie à 7.00*
9.   *Son père a construit une maison*
10. *Je n'ai rien fait*

Further Compound Tense sentences answers

1.   *Ils/elles étaient parti(e)s*
2.   *Mes amis auront ouvert le cadeau*
3.   *Elle aurait compris*
4.   *J'avais écrit la lettre*
5.   *Je t'aurais cru(e)*
6.   *Ils/elles auraient pu partir*
7.   *Tu n'avais rien dit*
8.   *Nous aurions lu le journal*
9.   *Elles seront retournées*
10. *Ses sœurs étaient tombées*

Compound Agreement sentences answers

I   Être verb agreement

1.   *Elle est arrivée à 6*
2.   *Les filles sont restées dans la maison*
3.   *Nous sommes partis après la pièce*
4.   *Elle serait allée au match*
5.   *Elles étaient tombées*

II   PDO – Object Pronouns

1.   *Nous les avons vus*
2.   *Je l'ai rencontrée à la gare*
3.   *Il les aurait aimées*
4.   *Tes livres ? Oui je les ai vendus*
5.   *Elle les avait comprises*

III   PDO – Object Antecedent in Relative construction

1.   *C'est une femme que j'ai rencontrée l'année dernière*
2.   *Ce sont des livres que j'avais lus*
3.   *Ce sont des problèmes que j'aurais compris*
4.   *Voici la fenêtre qu'il a cassée*
5.   *J'aime les histoires qu'il a écrites*

IV   PDO – Wh- object questions

1.   *Quelle fenêtre as-tu cassée ?*
2.   *Quels livres as-tu achetés ?*
3.   *Quel vin avez-vous préféré?*
4.   *Quelles filles as-tu rencontrées?*
5.   *Quels problèmes as-tu résolus?*

V   Reflexive agreement

1.   *Les garçons s'étaient levés à six*
2.   *Ils se sont vus dans le miroir*
3.   *Elle s'est envoyé une lettre (no PDO agreement here because s' is Indirect)*
4.   *Il se serait habillé*
5.   *La fille s'est surprise*

Tense Chart Sentences answers

1. *Je chante*
2. *Elle mange*
3. *Tu vends*
4. *Nous sommes allé(e)s*
5. *Ils ont parlé*
6. *Il apprend le français depuis trois ans*
7. *J'ai acheté un bateau hier*
8. *Nous allions à Brighton chaque samedi*
9. *Il faisait du soleil*
10. *Nous mangions le déjeuner*
11. *Je jouais du banjo*
12. *Elle avait fini le livre*
13. *Ils/elles avaient dormi*
14. *Il parlait depuis cinq minutes*
15. *Nous irons au théâtre demain*
16. *Vous arriverez dans dix minutes*
17. *Ils/elles comprendront*
18. *Il finirait à sept heures*
19. *Je serais très content*
20. *Je nagerais si.....*
21. *Nous les connaissons depuis des années*
22. *Quand je serai plus âgé(e) j'achèterai une moto*
23. *Ils/elles rentreront quand ils/elles auront fini leur travail*
24. *Quand nous sommes arrivé(e)s il était là depuis deux heures*
25. *Je parle depuis dix minutes*

Past Historic sentences answers

1. *He was surprised to see them*
2. *The duke entered the château*
3. *When they had eaten their meal, the pupils finished their homework*
4. *They saw them at the end of the road*
5. *She lost her handkerchief*
6. *As soon as they had arrived in the village, they came to the church*
7. *Suddenly they were cold*
8. *He heard the train whistling*
9. *Suddenly I saw an enormous bear*
10. *"Absolutely not!" he replied*

Passive sentences answers

1. *Il a été remarqué par tout le monde*
2. *Une lettre sera envoyée demain*
3. *La fenêtre a été cassée par l'explosion*
4. *La table avait été réparée par le menuisier*
5. *Nous serons accueillis par le maire*
6. *On leur a donné un livre (Passive not possible here because of original Indirect Object)*
7. *La porte s'est ouverte (Reflexive 'Passive')*
8. *On nous enverra l'information (original Indirect Object)*
9. *Ça ne se fait simplement pas (Reflexive 'Passive')*
10. *On lui a dit la bonne réponse (original Indirect Object)*

Imperative sentences answers
1. *Écrivez la lettre*
2. *Chante cette chanson*
3. *Finissons le film*
4. *Ne parle pas*
5. *Cache-les*
6. *Ne les cachez pas*
7. *Donne-moi le livre*
8. *Ne lui donne pas le livre*
9. *Lève-toi*
10. *Ne vous habillez pas*

Question sentences answers
1. *Parle-t-il français/Est-ce qu'il parle français?*
2. *Seras-tu à la boum/Est-ce que tu seras à la boum?*
3. *Est-ce que ta mère aime tes amis?*
4. *Quand es-tu arrivé(e)/Quand est-ce que tu es arrivé(e)?*
5. *Quels livres as-tu aimés/quels livres est-ce que tu as aimés?*
6. *Pourquoi seront-ils au repas/Pourquoi est-ce qu'ils seront au repas?*
7. *À qui as-tu envoyé le cadeau/À qui est-ce que tu as envoyé le cadeau?*
8. *Ont-elles aimé la pièce/Est-ce qu'elles ont aimé la pièce?*
9. *À quelle heure partiront-ils/À quelle heure est-ce qu'ils partiront?*
10. *Est-ce que ton frère regardait ce film?/ Ton frère, regardait-il ce film?*

Negative sentences answers
1. *Je ne sais pas*
2. *Il n'avait pas fini*
3. *Nous n'irons pas en vacances cette année*
4. *Mes parents n'ont pas compris le problème*
5. *Je n'ai pas de sœur*
6. *Je ne sais rien*
7. *Je n'ai jamais voyagé en Italie*
8. *Nous n'avons que 30 Euros*
9. *Personne ne comprend*
10. *Rien n'est important*

Verbs and Infinitives sentences answers
1. *Nous avons essayé de comprendre*
2. *Je préfère pêcher*
3. *Mon père a décidé d'acheter cette maison*
4. *Il semble comprendre le problème*
5. *J'ai demandé à mon prof d'expliquer la question*
6. *Il a refusé d'essayer de cesser de fumer*
7. *Nous devons partir maintenant*
8. *Elle s'est décidée à essayer d'apprendre l'allemand*
9. *J'espère aller en Italie pendant l'été*
10. *Il nous a dit d'arriver à 7.00*

Reflexive verb sentences answers

1. *Elle s'est blessée*
2. *Nous nous amuserons*
3. *Nous nous sommes acheté des cadeaux*
4. *Ils se connaissent*
5. *Ce vin se boit avec du bœuf*
6. *Cela se comprend*
7. *Il s'occupe des invités*
8. *Elle s'est moquée du prof*
9. *Tu te couperas le doigt*
10. *Il s'est lavé le visage*

Subjunctive sentences answers

1. *Il faut que nous mangions à 7.00*
2. *Bien que ce soit un voyage court ,....*
3. *Il semble qu'ils/elles comprennent*
4. *Ils/elles attendent que nous partions*
5. *Je veux que tu partes maintenant*
6. *Ils/elles l'ont acheté sans que nous le sachions*
7. *Je suis désolé(e) que tu vendes la maison*
8. *Elle est la meilleure chanteuse que je connaisse*
9. *Je suis content que tu sois là*
10. *Ils/elles veulent que je devienne président*
11. *Il est content que j'aie fini le livre*
12. *Il semble qu'ils/elles aient compris*
13. *Bien qu'elle l'ait rencontré,...*
14. *C'est le meilleur vin que j'aie goûté*
15. *Je suis désolé que tu ne l'aies pas vue*

Modal sentences answers

1. *Ils/Elles veulent comprendre*
2. *Elle avait voulu partir à 7*
3. *Ils/Elles devraient lire le livre*
4. *Tu pourras finir à l'heure*
5. *Il a dû la/le laisser dans la voiture*
6. *Nous aurions pu regarder la pièce*
7. *J'aurais dû laver le plancher*
8. *Elle aurait dû réserver la chambre*
9. *Nous devions/avons dû écrire un essai (this could either be a single event or a regular event)*
10. *Il aurait pu nous avertir du danger*

Y Avoir answers

1.   *Il y avait une école ici*
2.   *Il y aura des problèmes*
3.   *Soudain il y a eu un bruit fort*
4.   *Il y aurait eu beaucoup de gens*
5.   *Il doit y avoir une boulangerie près d'ici*
6.   *Il pourrait y avoir un problème*
7.   *Il y aurait une bonne raison pour cela*
8.   *Il y a beaucoup de pommes*
9.   *Il y aura eu beaucoup de bruit*
10. *Il faut qu'il y ait une solution (or 'Il doit y avoir une solution')*

Conditional structure sentences answers

1.   *Si tu ne rentres pas maintenant il y aura des problèmes*
2.   *Nous achèterions la maison si nous avions assez d'argent*
3.   *Si tu écris à ta tante elle te donnera de l'argent*
4.   *Si tu avais écouté tu aurais compris*
5.   *Tu aurais pu partir à l'heure si tu t'étais levé(e) tôt*
6.   *Si tu étais arrivé(e) à six heures nous aurions mangé ensemble*
7.   *Nous serons contents si tu gagnes*
8.   *Si tu étais parti(e) à l'heure, tu serais arrivé(e) avant le début du match*
9.   *Si tu veux nous finirons bientôt*
10. *Si tu apprends tout ceci, tu réussiras*

Miscellaneous constructions answers

Present participles and après avoir/être + past participle

1.   *Des résultats surprenants (adjective use)*
2.   *Un voyage fatiguant (adjective use)*
3.   *Une fille intéressante (adjective use)*
4.   *Je les ai découverts mangeant du chocolat*
5.   *Il a ouvert la porte parlant bruyamment*
6.   *J'ai mangé le gâteau en lisant le journal*
7.   *Ayant parlé à sa sœur il est rentré*
8.   *Après avoir fini le dîner, ils ont regardé la télé*
9.   *Étant arrivée elle a téléphoné à sa mère*
10. *Après avoir fini le travail je suis allé au bar*
     (These last four could have alternative forms. See Chapter 2 section 11.1)

Il y a, venir de, être en train de, être sur le point de, depuis construction

1.   *J'y travaillais il y a sept ans*
2.   *Elle a commencé son travail il y a deux semaines*
3.   *Ils viennent de finir*
4.   *Nous venions de manger quand le prêtre est arrivé*
5.   *Je suis en train de parler*
6.   *Il était en train de jouer au golf quand il a plu*
7.   *Nous sommes sur le point de partir*
8.   *Elles étaient sur le point de s'endormir*
9.   *J'enseigne ici depuis vingt-cinq ans*
10. *Elle dormait depuis trois heures*

Subject and object pronouns answers

1. *Elle le connaît*
2. *Ils/Elles nous aiment*
3. *Nous leur avons raconté une histoire*
4. *Je la lui ai vendue*
5. *Tes parents? Je ne les ai pas vus*
6. *L'as-tu rencontrée?*
7. *Fais-le maintenant!*
8. *Regarde-moi!*
9. *Ne me le dis pas!*
10. *J'en suis content*
11. *Venir à la boum? Je ne les y ai pas invités*
12. *Nous y sommes allées l'année dernière*
13. *Prends encore du fromage! Non merci j'en ai déjà assez pris*
14. *Voici un verre de vin. Oui, j'en voudrais (un)*
15. *Il les y a laissés*
16. *Elle le lui a donné hier*
17. *Nous lui en avons déjà envoyé*
18. *Il nous les a offertes*
19. *J'y ai réfléchi*
20. *Nous leur enverrons les clefs.*

Emphatic, strong or stressable pronouns answers

1. *Avec eux*
2. *Pour elle*
3. *Après lui*
4. *Près de moi*
5. *Lève-toi!*
6. *Montre-moi ton passeport*
7. *Dis-moi la vérité*
8. *Ne me dis pas la vérité*
9. ***Lui?*** *C'est un idiot/il est idiot*
10. *C'était elles qui étaient arrivées les premières*
11. *Ils l'ont fait eux-mêmes*
12. *Il est plus intelligent que toi*
13. *Elle est meilleure que lui*
14. *Ma famille et moi sommes ravis*
15. *Elle est moi l'avons acheté*

Relative pronouns answers

Basic relative structures in French

1. *L'homme que j'ai rencontré était vieux*
2. *Le vin que j'aime beaucoup est de Bordeaux*
3. *La chose qui m'a surpris était ses cheveux*
4. *C'est un problème qui m'agace*
5. *Ce que je préfère c'est la pêche*
6. *Ce qui m'agace le plus c'est la gourmandise*
7. *Un écureuil est un rat qui vit dans les arbres*
8. *Je ne sais pas ce que vous voulez dire*
9. *Dis-moi ce qui s'est passé*
10. *Elle est quelqu'un que je respecte beaucoup*

More complex relatives in French

1. *La chose dont j'étais le plus heureux était le déjeuner*
2. *C'est quelque chose dont je ne comprends pas l'importance*
3. *C'est un animal dont j'ai peur*
4. *C'est un homme pour qui j'ai un grand respect*
5. *Ce sont des gens pour qui je ferais n'importe quoi*
6. *Elle est la dame à qui j'ai donné mon livre*
7. *La musique est quelque chose sans laquelle je ne peux pas vivre*
8. *Voici le bureau où je travaille*
9. *Un tonneau est un conteneur dans lequel nous versons de la bière*
10. *C'est le moment après lequel ils partent tous.*

Interrogative, Demonstrative, Possessive and Indefinite pronouns answers

1. *Qu'as-tu fait ?/Qu'est-ce que tu as fait ?*
2. *Qui a fait ça ?/Qui est-ce qui a fait ça ?*
3. *Qu'as-tu acheté hier?/Qu'est-ce que tu as acheté hier ?*
4. *As-tu lu ces livres ? Lequel préfères-tu ?/Lequel est-ce que tu préfères ?*
5. *Lesquelles/laquelle de ces pommes aimes-tu ?/ Lesquelles/laquelle de ces pommes est-ce que tu aimes ?*
6. *De toutes ses pièces, celle-ci est ma favorite*
7. *Ces arbres sont plus grands que ceux-là*
8. *Ce bâtiment-ci est plus vieux que celui-là*
9. *Quand je me sers d'un stylo, je choisis toujours celui-ci*
10. *As-tu utilisé ce manteau ou celui-là ?*
11. *Peindre les fenêtres. Oh J'adore ça/cela*
12. *Ça/cela va mieux maintenant.*
13. *Ceci est important*
14. *Cela/ça me fait rire!*
15. *Ceci est ce que je ne comprends pas.*
16. *J'aime cette maison mais je préfère la mienne*
17. *Ses photos sont plus intéressantes que les siennes*
18. *Notre prof est ennuyeux mais as-tu entendu le leur ?*
19. *Ce gâteau est à moi*
20. *C'est à elle et non pas à toi!*

Adjective phrases and sentences answers

1. *L'avocat était malhonnête*
2. *Un avocat malhonnête*
3. *Une vieille maison*
4. *Un enfant heureux*
5. *Un petit enfant*
6. *La robe verte*
7. *L'ancien président*
8. *Un bâtiment ancien*
9. *Mes propres parents*
10. *Un nouvel appartement*
11. *Une vie heureuse*
12. *Une chemise bleu clair*
13. *Une histoire plus passionnante*
14. *Une meilleure solution*
15. *Le pire problème*
16. *Il (c') est difficile de comprendre la chimie*
17. *Oui c'est difficile à comprendre*
18. *Il (c') est important de travailler dur*
19. *Oui' c'est important*
20. *Il est facile à comprendre*

Adverbs and Articles answers

1. *Elle a parlé très clairement*
2. *Ils/elles parlent le français couramment*
3. *Mon père conduit lentement*
4. *Il était énormément grand*
5. *Ils/elles sont probablement là*
6. *Il a réagi de façon intelligente*
7. *J'aime les romans*
8. *Le gazole est le carburant le plus populaire*
9. *L'allemand est difficile*
10. *La coopération est essentielle*
11. *Ma mère s'est coupé le doigt*
12. *Il s'est coupé les cheveux*
13. *Je ne travaille jamais le dimanche*
14. *As-tu de la monnaie?*
15. *Voudrais-tu de la bière?*
16. *Il a de la patience*
17. *Voudrais-tu un verre de bière?*
18. *Elle a beaucoup de talent*
19. *Est-ce que je peux avoir un des livres que tu as achetés?*
20. *Je n'ai pas de frère*
21. *Ils/elles n'ont pas de chance*
22. *Sa mère était danseuse*
23. *Mon fils est devenu dompteur de lions*
24. *Son père est avocat*
25. *Son père est avocat*

Bibliography

Bryne L.S.R. and Churchill E.L. Revised and rewritten by Glanville Price (1993) A Comprehensive French Grammar (4th Edition), Oxford, Blackwell

Detey S., Durand J., Laks B. and Lyche C. (2010) Les variétés du Français Parlé dans l'Espace Francophone, Paris, Éditions OPHRYS

Hawkins R. and Towell R. (2015) French Grammar and Usage (4th Edition), London and New York, Routledge

Rouayrenc C. (2010) Le Français Oral, 2 Volumes, Paris, Belin

Index

Lightning Source UK Ltd.
Milton Keynes UK
UKHW021409131021
392145UK00008B/1642